Winslow Homer and His Cullercoats Paintings

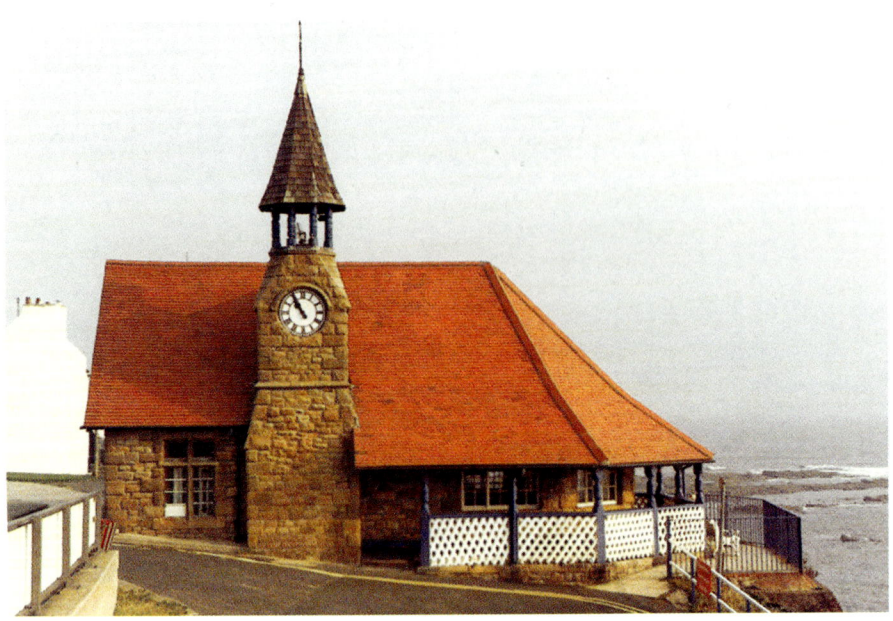

The Watch House, Cullercoats, 2017.
Photograph by Cleota Reed.

Winslow Homer

AND HIS

CULLERCOATS
PAINTINGS

*An American Artist in
England's North East*

DAVID TATHAM

SYRACUSE UNIVERSITY PRESS

Copyright © 2021 by Syracuse University Press
Syracuse, New York 13244-5290

All Rights Reserved

First Edition 2021
21 22 23 24 25 26   6 5 4 3 2 1

∞ The paper used in this publication meets the minimum requirements of the American National Standard for Information Sciences—Permanence of Paper for Printed Library Materials, ANSI Z39.48-1992.

For a listing of books published and distributed by Syracuse University Press, visit https://press.syr.edu.

ISBN: 978-0-8156-3700-4 (hardcover)
        978-0-8156-1130-1 (paperback)

Library of Congress Control Number: 2021931100

Manufactured in the United States of America

For Cleota

———————

And in Memory of
Lucretia Hoover Giese

Contents

LIST OF ILLUSTRATIONS   *ix*

ACKNOWLEDGMENTS   *xi*

1. Introduction   *1*

2. Homer as a "New Artist"   *7*

3. England's North East   *11*

4. Homer's Cullercoats   *17*

5. Fishwives   *25*

6. On and above the Sands   *47*

7. Storm   *53*

8. Beyond the Village   *59*

9. Culmination   *66*

10. Aftermath   *74*

NOTES   *81*

BIBLIOGRAPHY   *87*

INDEX   *89*

Illustrations

Color Plates

At the head of each chapter in which one or more of the following illustrations (plates) is discussed, the caption for each work includes the identification number (G&G) used in the five volumes of Lloyd Goodrich and Abigail Booth Gerdts, *Record of Works by Winslow Homer*, New York, 2005–2014.

(following page 33)

1. *Men Beaching a Boat*, 1881–1882
2. *Watching from the Cliffs*, 1881
3. *Four Fishwives*, 1881
4. *Homecoming*, 1883
5. *Fisherfolk on the Beach at Cullercoats*, 1881
6. *Beach Scene, Cullercoats*, 1881
7. *The Breakwater, Cullercoats*, 1882
8. *The Lookout*, 1882
9. *Perils of the Sea*, 1881
10. *Watching the Tempest*, 1881
11. *The Gale*, 1883–1893
12. *Coursing the Hare*, 1882–1883
13. *Bridlington Quay*, 1883
14. *Hark! The Lark*, 1882
15. *A Voice from the Cliffs*, 1883
16. *The Incoming Tide*, 1883
17. *Inside the Bar*, 1883
18. *Returning Fishing Boats*, 1883

19. *An Afterglow*, 1883
20. *The Life Line*, 1884

Maps

Map 1. Homer's Cullercoats   *16*
Map 2. Newcastle upon Tyne   *23*

Acknowledgments

AMONG THE MANY PERSONS in England and America who have aided my work on this study, I am grateful to Hazel Fleming for introducing me to the remarkable resources of Newcastle's Literary and Philosophical Society (locally known as "The Lit and Phil"). It is home to one of England's oldest, largest, and most interesting independent libraries. I thank its librarian, Kay Easson, for providing information regarding William Adamson's association with the society while Homer resided in Cullercoats. Among others who aided my research in the county of Northumberland, I am much obliged to Isabel Keating of Collections and Archives, the Northumberland Estates Office, Alnwick, for her helpful response to my inquiries relating to possible visits by Homer to Alnwick Castle, its grounds, and its nearby fishing streams. No such visits are recorded.

For enlightenment concerning the history of Newcastle and its surrounding towns and villages, my thanks go to members of the ever-helpful staffs of the Tyne and Wear Archives; the Whitley Bay Library; the North Shields Library; the City Library of Newcastle; and Newcastle's Great North Museum: Hancock. In London, the National Art Library's collections and staff have as always provided rapid access to a wealth of secondary sources.

On a visit to Cullercoats in 1984 with my wife, Cleota Reed, we were joined by Tony Harrison, who had resided in the village with his family for many years while commuting to Newcastle. Harrison introduced us to the elderly Cuthbert (Cud) Simpson, who reminisced at length about his grandparents' recollections of the village in Homer's time and about local Homer lore as he recalled it. Harrison also led us on an instructive tour of the topography of Cullercoats in relation to Homer's paintings. Harrison's *Winslow Homer in England* (2004) provided the first compact illustrated survey of the artist's most important Cullercoats paintings, many of them reproduced in color.[1]

I am indebted as well to the work of Tony Knipe, organizer of the landmark exhibition of 1988, *Winslow Homer: All the Cullercoats Pictures*, mounted in Sunderland at the Northern Centre for Contemporary Art (the "All" of the title means "limited to"). The exhibition was the first to consider comprehensively, in depth, and with important insights Homer's Cullercoats work. The review of the exhibition by the art historian and critic for the *Manchester Guardian*, Tim Hilton, remains a major assessment of Homer's career-long strengths and significance as an artist.

I have gleaned much concerning Homer in England from Elizabeth Athens, Randall Bond, Sarah Burns, Mary Ann Calo, John Carbonell, Jana Colacino, Helen Cooper, the late Lucretia Hoover Giese, Peter R. Hornby, Domenic Iacono, Patricia Junker, Roy Parkinson, Sue Reed, Mark Simpson, Stephanie Loeb Stepanek, and Judith Walsh among many others. I owe special thanks to David Oakey and also to Franca Candrian for their valuable help in locating an important painting.

Cleota joins me in thanking longtime friends for hospitality during our often indirect routes from London to or from Newcastle and Cullercoats. These include Peter Cormack and Sandra Coley of London; Mary and Jim Cox of New Pitsligo, Scotland; Cathy Huggins and the late Tony Herbert of Shrewsbury, Shropshire; and Malcolm and Diana Whitaker of Harcombe Farm, Syde, Gloucestershire and their good neighbors at the village's historic chantry, Chad and Norma Doveton. Closer to home in Syracuse, the ever-resourceful Edward Alan Gokey of Syracuse University's Bird Library has once again aided the progress of my research concerning Homer. William Bowen of the university's Department of Art and Music Histories has been of great help in keeping the many tasks of manuscript preparation in order.

Lee McTighe has enlightened me concerning Homer and his family's associations with West Townsend, Massachusetts and its close neighbor, New Ipswich, New Hampshire. I thank Lucy Person and Heila Martin of Legacy Graphics for their locus map designs. Ragen Martin Tiliakos has as always been a splendid companion for Cleota and myself in Boston, Syracuse, and London.

As so regularly in the past Cleota has generously taken time from her own scholarly studies to critique her husband's drafts, steadily asking the right questions and suggesting with happy frequency that it must be time for us to slip away to London or Madrid. I tip my cap as ever to grandchildren and great grandchildren who have enlivened my labors. In my earlier studies of Homer's work I have expressed thanks to Lloyd Goodrich (1897–1987) for his early encouragement. I now do so again, mindful that in our last discussion at the Whitney Museum he observed that much work still remained to be done concerning Homer in England. His assessment continues to be valid.

Over the course of half a century four ophthalmologists—the late Dr. Theodore Smith and Drs. John Hoepner, George Spaeth, and Steven Trotter Simmons—have brought their great expertise to the task of keeping my vision bright, enabling me to continue to see not only what Winslow Homer had drawn and painted but much else in the world around me. My gratitude is unbounded.

Members of the staff of Syracuse University Press have with constant good cheer provided much excellent advice, professional wisdom, and patience. In this, my fifth and final study for the press regarding key aspects of Homer's career, I again thank them heartily.

Syracuse
November 2019

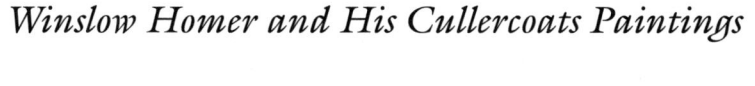

Winslow Homer and His Cullercoats Paintings

I

Introduction

THE EIGHTEEN MONTHS (1881–1882) that the American artist Winslow Homer spent in England in the Northumbrian village of Cullercoats proved to be one of the most interesting, adventurous, and productive periods of his long career. Little documentation of this overseas episode survives other than his Cullercoats paintings, but these constitute a rich pictorial account of his thinking and activity while in the village and related sites. By giving close attention to some of the most ambitious of Homer's Cullercoats paintings, the present study seeks to cast new light on their maker's experiences in England's North East region, an often misunderstood period in his development. Much if not most of Homer's Cullercoats work has tended to remain little known in both England and America.

When Homer sailed to England in March 1881, he was already well established as a leading member of his generation of American painters. Critics in the American art press had occasionally referred to him as the "most American of American painters," a description that coupled praise with an implication that his work was also to some degree provincial compared to that of the more distinguished of his European-trained American contemporaries.

Almost immediately following his arrival in Cullercoats, Homer set aside most elements that had characterized his American paintings. He formed instead what may be considered his "Cullercoats manner." In 1883, when a substantial group of his paintings from the village first reached exhibition in New York, one critic described them as the products of a "new artist." Homer's Cullercoats experience had in a sense initiated a sequence of periodic renewals that would continue for the rest of his career.

When Homer sailed for England on March 14, 1881 he was forty-five years old. He had not previously been to any part of the British Isles. His only earlier time in Europe had been in 1866–1867 when he spent ten months in and around Paris.[1] He disembarked at Liverpool on March 26 and traveled by rail directly to London. There he lodged for three weeks in a historic artists' quarter within the borough of Marylebone.[2] After this introduction to the great city, he traveled north some 290 miles to the county of Northumberland and its village of Cullercoats by the North Sea. He settled there for what would become a year and a half of little other than intensive painting and drawing. His finished work included almost a hundred watercolors of various sizes and subjects, all distinctly different from his earlier work in the medium. They differed as well from whatever he may have seen of British painting up to that time.

Perhaps the first thing to be observed about Homer's time in England's North East region is how quickly and thoroughly he bonded with the locale. The village of Cullercoats with its spacious bay and long-established community of fisherfolk had over the years occasionally attracted British artists of note for brief visits. None of them left so interesting or illuminating a record of the life of the village as Homer did through his watercolors, nearly all of them figural subjects. In addition to these paintings, he made fifty or so exhibition drawings of great strengths as well as a few highly interesting oil paintings, leaving some of the latter works unfinished. So far as is known, none of his Cullercoats work remains in the United Kingdom. Homer shipped nearly all of it to New York in advance of his return to the city in November 1882.

In January 1883, an exhibition of four of his Cullercoats watercolors in New York won exceptionally high praise from art critics, art dealers, and the general public (this exhibition is discussed in more detail in chapter 9). Soon afterward, however, his newer paintings of other subjects and locations rapidly drew attention away from what he had achieved in Cullercoats.

With Homer's death in 1910, the unsold portion of his work remained in New York in the care of his elder brother Charles Homer Jr. and from then on was little seen. With Charles's death in 1917, many of these watercolors entered the art market and revived a degree of interest in the Cullercoats subjects. Not until the twenty-first century, however, could one safely assume that nearly all of Homer's Cullercoats paintings and drawings were known and recorded. (The five volumes of Lloyd Goodrich and Abigail Booth Gerdts's *Record of Works by Winslow Homer* contain the basic data.)

While selections of the Cullercoats watercolors have regularly found appreciative audiences when shown in museum exhibitions, relatively little about them has reached print. Indeed, for nearly a century, scholarly and popular biographies of Homer have often referred to his year and a half in England merely as his "turning point," often saying little if anything about the paintings he had produced during his stay there. The authors' and critics' use of the phrase "turning point" applied to this period of Homer's work seemed in a sense to excuse them from observing the substance of what Homer had painted while in Cullercoats. Then too, because "turning" may imply impermanence, the phrase in Homer's case has worked against expectations of qualities of lasting interest in the paintings.

Further confusion relating to the phrase "turning point" has risen from the lack of a common understanding of precisely what the phrase might mean in Homer's case. His first two biographers, William Howe Downes in 1911 and Lloyd Goodrich in 1944, made use of the phrase in two quite different ways. For Downes, Homer's American work prior to his time in England had drawn comments from critics ranging from derision (rare) to modest praise (common). With the first exhibition of his Cullercoats work in 1883, however, positive critical response rose to a high level and with rare exceptions remained there for the rest of his career. For Downes, then, Homer's "turning" was a reception-based matter.

Goodrich interpreted the phrase much more broadly. "In every way the Tynemouth [i.e., Cullercoats] experience marked a turning point in Homer's career . . . [with] a phenomenal maturing in mind and vision . . . and a long step forward in technical mastery. . . . It settled in his mind the kind of life he wanted to lead and the kind of art he wanted to produce." Goodrich's definition became in many respects the basis for most later scholarly and popular references to a "turning point" in Homer studies.[3]

By the 1940s the phrase had become a commonplace that divided accounts of Homer's career into two dissimilar parts. The first included his subjects from American towns and rural, rustic, and seaside life as he had observed it from the mid-1860s to 1880. The second part consisted of his post-Cullercoats years, 1884–1910, as America's "great painter of the sea." This bifurcation of his career had the unfortunate result of isolating his Cullercoats work, leaving it as little more than a hinge connecting the two major periods but belonging to neither. The Cullercoats paintings became categorized as transitional works, products of a foreign interval that had interrupted Homer's otherwise American-based, American-influenced, and American-interpreted career.

Yet from the beginning of his time in the village, what Homer painted and how he painted it had broken sharply from his American manner up to that point. Further, after he had returned to the United States in 1882, scarcely any aspect of what he had painted in Cullercoats contributed to what he would accomplish in the years that followed. The Cullercoats paintings are best seen as an independent body of work of significant though idiosyncratic strengths.

Perhaps because these paintings have come to be categorized as works of transition, they have tended to escape rigorous examination or even accurate description of their contents. As a result, misinformation about their subjects has established itself in numerous accounts of Homer's career. Cullercoats has steadily been characterized simply as a "fishing village," though it had neither docks nor a fish market. Well over half its residents had nothing to do with fishing.

Then too, American publications have at times referred to the Cullercoats fisherfolk as "peasants" or "peasant-like," even though this characterization is grossly incorrect. Neither the fisherfolk whom Homer knew and painted, nor their forebears as far back as the mid-eighteenth century, were in any respect peasants.[4]

A further contribution to confusion has come from writers who have assumed that because Cullercoats sits at the edge of the occasionally stormy North Sea, it was here that Homer was awakened to the great power of the oceans. But well before his time in England he had experienced the many varied and often grand moods of the Atlantic from New Jersey to Maine.

Popular and scholarly publications concerning Homer have described Cullercoats as a storm-ridden location, but there is little or no basis for such a reputation in weather records. Cornwall in England's South West region has traditionally held a well-established reputation as the English region more prone to storms than any other. These and other inaccuracies in published accounts of Homer in England have tended to distort what from all evidence he experienced in Cullercoats.

The singularity of Homer's Cullercoats work was not unique. His "Reconstruction" oils of the mid-1870s had also broken sharply from his established manner of the time. In that instance he again concentrated almost exclusively on a subject wholly new to him: African American life in postemancipation Virginia. He did so in a sequence of distinctly original and deeply serious oil paintings that treated this controversial subject movingly and with great insight. He did so in a new manner, one to which he would not return once he had left Virginia. Like his Reconstruction paintings, Homer's Cullercoats work remains outside most mainstream accounts of his achievements. Yet by any measure it enlarges and enriches his significance as a major American artist.

If Homer's time in England is to be considered a turning point, it needs to be considered within the context of the other major turnings of his long career, for he was almost never quite the same artist for long. The first of these shifts, often overlooked, came with his redefinition of himself as an artist in the early 1860s, when he ceased to be only a freelance graphic illustrator much in demand by the national pictorial press and established himself also as a painter in oils. This quickly brought him to prominence in the American fine art community as a distinctly "homegrown" rather than Continent-trained painter. No other American artist of his time succeeded in making this leap from the relatively confined realm of black-and-white illustration for popular publications to high standing in the wholly different realm of painting subjects of his own choosing in colors. With that turn Homer made himself an independent and successful fine artist. For more than a decade he remained also a well-paid freelance graphic artist, drawing original subjects for the popular press to earn what was needed to maintain his professional studio as a painter.

Another turning point was his adoption in the early 1870s of watercolor as a second medium. This dual proficiency made him something of a rarity among master American painters, most of whom worked primarily if not exclusively in oils. A third turning point came in 1878 when during his summer at Houghton Farm in the Hudson Valley he produced an extensive group of watercolors of young shepherdesses, at times dressing them in eighteenth-century costumes more suitable for the stage than the meadow. In these he began to alter his usual naturalism to gain an inventiveness, freshness, and lyric sense new to his work. Echoes of his Houghton Farm experience returns quietly here and there within his Cullercoats watercolors.

Homer in the 1860s and 1870s had progressively broadened his identity as an artist. He would continue to do so following his return from England and his subsequent move to Prout's Neck on the coast of Maine. In each of these enlargements of his identity, early and late, his proficiency and originality as an artist grew.

The chapters that follow seek to cast useful light on what Homer accomplished while in England's North East. They look closely at the paintings rather than to the relatively small body of literature that concerns them. The chapters proceed from an assumption that English painting of Homer's generation had little if any influence on him before or during his time in Cullercoats. Chapters 2 through 4 offer a gathering of background information from what little is known of his life in Cullercoats. Chapter 2 moves ahead in time to take note of the glowing reception his Cullercoats paintings received in New York when they were first exhibited. This established Homer more solidly than ever before as a major American artist. It also gave serious observers reason to wonder what in England, and in Cullercoats in particular, played a part in bringing this change about. Chapters 5 through 9 consist of readings of what Homer painted, touching only as needed on the circumstances of their making. The commentary gives little attention to comparative studies of Homer with other artists, for this mode of inquiry accomplishes little when an artist is by instinct and practice so strongly and distinctly individualistic as was Homer. His development had always been little planned and involuntary. It remained so in Cullercoats.

2

Homer as a "New Artist"

IN JANUARY 1883, the American Watercolor Society mounted its six-teenth annual exhibition of new work by artist members, which was held at the National Academy in Manhattan. This annual showing had become one of the city's more important fine art events. The 1883 showing included four of Homer's Cullercoats subjects, all painted specifically for this exhibition.[1] Each of the four dealt with some aspect of the intimate relationship between Cullercoats fisherfolk and the sea. The most prominent of the figures in the paintings by far were those of Cullercoats fishwives.

The American press reviews of the first exhibition of Homer's Cullercoats paintings left scarcely any doubt about the importance of this body of work in his career. A summary of these reviews shows how suddenly Homer's stat-ure as an artist rose among American critics and how clearly those critics had begun to comprehend his new aims and strengths as they appeared in the Cullercoats watercolors.

Reviewers of the 1883 exhibition in the art press showered all four of Homer's paintings with high praise. Typical of the enthusiasm was that of the usually conservative critic of the *New York Evening World*, whose unflag-gingly positive review included these insights:

> He gives us some large drawings [i.e., watercolors] of English fisherwomen which are no longer studies or character sketches or *genre* pictures, but which touch a far higher plane. They are pictures in the fullest sense, and to charac-terize them properly one must fall back on an old-time expression. . . . They are works of High Art. They have an ideal element.[2]

The most perceptive and polished of the critics, Marianna Van Rensselaer (1851–1935), had followed Homer's work closely for several years, disliking and sharply criticizing much of it. Now however she championed what she had seen in the exhibition. She claimed that his time in England had transformed him into nothing less than a "new artist" and a most impressive one. She wrote:

7

The hero of the hour was unquestionably Mr. Winslow Homer. For once everyone whose vote told for much gave it for the same candidate. . . . To say that each and all of his [four paintings] were individual conceptions is implied in the fact that they were painted by Mr. Homer, for he has never at any time done a stroke which could have been credited to any other man. . . . They were more than fine, these pictures of Mr. Homer's. They were powerful both in their originality and in the sort of dignified beauty they secured. Everything else in the [exhibition] room, almost, was killed by their strong presence.[3]

After Van Rensselaer had examined more of Homer's Cullercoats paintings, she wrote a longer and more detailed appreciation of what he had done in an article published in the November 1883 issue of *The Century,* a well-respected journal of culture. Her article, which was the most attentive, detailed, and affirmative professional consideration of Homer's Cullercoats work by any critic up to that time, remains a major document in the history of the reception of Homer's work. Among Van Rensselaer's new observations were these:

It is proof of his true artistic instinct and insight, and his freedom from conventionality of thought, that Mr. Homer, who had so clearly understood and expressed the American type during so many years of working, could now free himself so entirely from its memory so as to make these English girls as distinctly, as typically, English as any which have ever come from a British hand. It is this most recent phase of Mr. Homer's work . . . [that] seem[s] to me not only [to include] . . . the most complete and beautiful things he has yet produced, but among the most interesting American art has yet created.

And later in the same review she wrote:

We are tempted to feel . . . that upon this unconventional, un-academic accent of his brush depends something of the interest, if not the value, of his work. Perhaps it is *because* of his *naiveté,* his occasional *gaucheries,* his sturdy if angular independence . . . that his handling seems so fresh, so unaffected, so peculiarly his own, so well adapted to the nature of the feeling it reveals.

And later still:

That he will give us many different kinds of work in the years to come, no one who has followed his course thus far can greatly doubt. And I am equally sure that it will be work that while keeping all his early independence of mood and freshness of vision, will show an ever-growing feeling for beauty, and an ever growing power to put it beautifully on canvas.[4]

The reviewers found no reason to suggest that in his Cullercoats paintings Homer might have shown influences from British art or artists. To say so would have been unnecessary, for Homer had already established himself in America as a markedly independent artist, one largely immune to the work of others. Nor did the reviewers suggest that Homer had carried from America to England any significant hallmark of his home manner. He was indeed a "new artist."

The reviews as a group made it seem clear enough that this change had occurred almost immediately following Homer's arrival in Cullercoats. There are no transitional paintings showing a process of adaptation from one distinct manner to another. As a painter Homer had always been an autodidact, a "natural" who worked from instinct and intuition rather than from instruction or example. He depended in good part on his exceptional powers of observation and an innate understanding of the nature of all that existed around him. This had enabled him to adapt with ease to new settings and to act quickly and surely. He did so throughout his career and especially so during his time in England.

He had few equals among his American colleagues in this respect. Fewer still had his quiet drive. In his Civil War paintings and those that soon followed he had shown himself in his profession to be, as the late art historian Lucretia Hoover Giese has aptly observed, "ambitious, competitive, and naturally experimental."[5] These qualities, accompanied by a personal manner of quiet reserve that persisted throughout his long career, contributed much to what he painted during his eighteen months in Cullercoats.

It is odd that the large body of paintings and drawings that he produced in Cullercoats has suffered such a long history of inadequate attention. The causes for this neglect are multiple and for the most part understandable. British scholars of the late nineteenth and twentieth centuries had no cause to interest themselves in the work of an artist visiting from abroad whose paintings had found no place in British public art collections. Then too, American scholars and others found it impractical or impossible to conduct research in England during the years of the Great Depression and World War II when persons who had known Homer in England were still alive. Curiously, in the 1950s, when it had again become a simple matter to visit Cullercoats, American scholars tended to study Homer's English sojourn from afar, seeking information about the village through correspondence with local Cullercoats historians. Some of what came from such inquiries has, alas, proven to be in various degrees inaccurate.

Homer himself and those who were closest to him left no significant body of papers relating to his time in the village or elsewhere in the region. This is hardly surprising in the case of an artist known to have been a man of few words both in conversation and on paper, and who at times seems to have viewed letters as a type of ephemera to be discarded once read. Consequently, the primary documents in the present study are Homer's Cullercoats paintings. They offer glimpses of his working environments, his closest associates, and the activities of the community in which he lived and worked. The paintings also say something about the man himself. Not least, they leave an impression that in the village of Cullercoats Homer was as pleased with where he was and what he was doing as he ever had been.

Of the village's more than fourteen hundred residents, the fisherfolk community, in whose neighborhood Homer resided, constituted perhaps five hundred persons. (The count varies widely from source to source depending on whom is counted, by whom, and when.) Most of the fisherfolk resided on streets close to Cullercoats Bay with its broad beach known as "the sands." Much of the sands was beyond the reach of ordinary high tides. This made it useful for the beaching of the community's flat-bottomed fishing boats known as "cobles." Homer seems certain to have chosen to reside close to the bay, which gave him easy access not only to sites where he would draw and paint but also to neighbors who were laboring men and women of a kind he had always respected.

The fisherfolk were in some ways an entity apart from the rest of the village's residents. A respectful separation between the two communities was in good part a function of their different ways of measuring time. The Cullercoats commuters, artisans, shopkeepers, clerks, laborers, artists, and others lived by the clock. The fisherfolk lived by the tides. This difference ordered the days and often the nights of each group and it did so in ways that were frequently poles apart. The two communities were further separated by the differing natures of their labors. Because fisherfolk men and women worked steadily outdoors, they needed to develop strong voices capable of carrying over distances on land as well as over water, and strong arms to regularly lift and carry substantial weights. The fishermen at times encountered dangerous weather at sea but were adept in avoiding it. The fishwives endured foul weather both on the sands and on village streets.

Homer, who in life as well as in his paintings, held skilled outdoor workers in high regard, surely earned the respect of the fisherfolk, for he worked as steadily and skillfully in his profession as did his neighbors in theirs. Though he aligned himself socially with both Cullercoats communities, he painted only the fisherfolk, and even then chiefly only the younger fishwives and fisherlasses. In all these ways he was indeed a "new artist."

3

England's North East

IT MAY SEEM CURIOUS that Homer in planning his time in England should have chosen to settle in England's North East. Most visiting artists of stature would have been inclined to locate themselves within or near London. That city was without question the historic and ever-vital center of Great Britain's world of art and artists. Homer's choice to live and work elsewhere suggests that well before crossing the Atlantic he had formed a location-specific agenda for what he meant to accomplish while abroad. It suggests as well that he believed himself to have no professional or personal need to associate himself with London or its art communities. He may have assumed that he would gain an adequate working introduction to the great city itself during his initial three weeks in England when he lodged in London, and this he seems to have done.

It has long been thought that during his time in the North East Homer occasionally returned to London to visit its museums and galleries or to otherwise take advantage of the city's great riches.[1] Yet his only documented return to the city occurred several months after he had settled in Cullercoats. The purpose of that trip was not to edify or entertain himself, but rather to deliver a new oil painting to the Royal Academy of Arts for inclusion in its forthcoming Summer Exhibition. This work was his oil painting *Hark! The Lark* (Plate 14), an image of younger Cullercoats fishwives momentarily entranced by the bird's flight and song. By this point Homer had ceased to be known in the village as a visiting American painter and had become instead a fixture of the community.[2]

Homer's productivity as a painter while in Cullercoats left little doubt that in this village he worked as intensively and successfully as he had at any time in his career as a painter. His work ethic in Cullercoats may have matched even that of the fisherfolk. During Homer's three weeks in London he had found time to visit the British Museum's department of prints and drawings, home also to its holdings of watercolors (then usually referred to as "drawings in color"). He had done so almost surely to acquaint himself with the museum's collection of historic and contemporary British paintings in the transparent watercolor medium. Having become the American master of this medium by the late 1870s, he would now work quite steadily in it throughout his Cullercoats stay. Among the medium's most distinguished historic masters had been J. M. W. Turner (1775–1851). His eminence had done much to inspire others in the United Kingdom and the United States to adopt this richer alternative to opaque watercolor.

The question of what brought Homer to live and paint in Cullercoats rather than elsewhere among England's many seaside locations has long inspired conjecture, but no well-documented answer to the question has yet arrived. One appeal of the village may have been that Cullercoats was home to a summer art colony. This meant if nothing more that providers of professional art supplies would be within easy reach. That Homer found the village satisfactory for his purposes is clear enough from the duration of his stay. While he apparently meant to spend only three months in Cullercoats before returning to New York, he found reason to alter this part of his plan and repeatedly prolonged his time in the village until its duration reached a total of eighteen months.[3]

Homer's reasons for extending his stay may have included the need to attend to one or more commissions. Sir Cecil Cochrane, nephew of Homer's Cullercoats patron William Cochrane, said in the 1940s that his uncle had once asked Homer to paint a local subject. Sir Cecil recalled that Homer had declined to do so on the grounds that he was already working on a commission for an American. No such commission is known, but a tradition to the effect that he had accepted one survived at least into the 1960s. It held that while in England Homer painted one or more local subjects for a New York businessman who was a "Son of Northumberland" and had sought painted images of his homeland.[4]

Whether Homer while in Cullercoats may have found interest in the history of the North East's rich cultural heritage is an unanswered question. Evidence of extensive ancient and medieval roots survived throughout the region. It ranged from the vast Hadrian's Wall to the ruins of various Roman buildings of many sizes, all attesting to long-lived settlements. Later, following the "dark" ages, the Anglo-Saxon occupation of the North East formed the geographic and political center of the Kingdom of Northumbria. In its prime Northumbria included not only the land that became the English counties of Northumberland and Durham, but also a large adjoining part of southeastern Scotland including Edinburgh. Durham's great medieval cathedral, less than ten miles south of Newcastle, was and remains evidence of Christianity's great spread and power in the North East during medieval times. Little if any of this touched Homer's work except for his distant depiction of the medieval ruins atop Tynemouth's great headland in his *Breakwater, Cullercoats* (Plate 7).

In the course of the eleventh century the name "Northumbria" gradually gave way to the appellation "Northumberland." Both names meant lands north of the River Humber with its great tidal estuary. In separating Yorkshire from its southern neighbor, Lincolnshire, the Humber served another purpose as well. It marked a conceptual divide between the North East of England, a region ever aware of its history as an independent kingdom, and the London-dominated South of England. In the North a sense of regional self-confidence and independence survived from the age of Northumbria into Homer's time (and many would say that such a sense still exists). Homer himself quite likely found this local spirit of reasoned independence from central authority to be agreeable, as he himself had little deep regard for those who represented authority in the world of art.

Soon after he had settled in Cullercoats he would have become aware of the practical importance of nobility in the locality. The hereditary 6th Duke of Northumberland, Algernon George Percy, whom Homer may have met, had played a vital role in the region's general welfare. He had commissioned the building of an additional church in Cullercoats, doing so in part to accommodate the village's steadily growing population. Construction on the Church of St. George, dedicated as a memorial to the 5th Duke, began in 1882 while Homer was still in the village. This impressive Gothic Revival structure of stone, designed by the eminent British architect John Loughborough Pearson, reached completion in 1884. Pearson situated the church close to neighboring Tynemouth's Long Sands beach with its expansive open view of the sea. He gave the church's tower an exceptionally tall spire to serve as a navigational guide for Cullercoats fishermen.[5]

In medieval times, the visual arts related to sacred subjects had flourished around the outpouring of the River Tyne, not far from where centuries later Cullercoats came to be. During the Victorian era, however, Northumbrian artists produced relatively little that amounted to more than skillful restatements of what flourished in London. It is fair to suppose that when Homer resided in Cullercoats he was in many respects the most original and accomplished artist in Northumberland, though always an outsider.

In the 1880s many of the village's residents were commuters. Some traveled by rail to jobs in and around Newcastle. Others went by rail to the Port of Tyne, three miles down the coast. The North Eastern Railway (NER), perhaps the country's most advanced and innovative line, connected these and many other points in the region. In 1882 the NER built a new and enlarged station near the center of Cullercoats. This replaced the earlier station of 1864, which, located in the southern part of the village, had become increasingly inconvenient as the village's population swelled. Homer is certain to have known both stations well.

Before leaving Cullercoats for New York, Homer may have had or sought opportunities to discuss with his village friends and acquaintances something that he and they had long held in common. This was a close knowledge of and deep respect for the internationally celebrated Italian military hero and world public figure, Giuseppe Garibaldi (1807–1882). His death in Italy on June 2, 1882, while Homer was in Cullercoats, almost certainly became a widespread topic of conversation throughout England's North East. At least a few who lived in or near Cullercoats and the other Tyneside communities would have remembered crowding into one or another of the several public addresses Garibaldi had made to huge audiences during his three weeks in London in the spring of 1860.

For three weeks in 1864, even more residents of Cullercoats and its neighboring communities would have watched with much interest Garibaldi's brig, *Commonwealth*, resting at anchor offshore Tynemouth while Garibaldi visited sites on or near the coast. He made many of these visits at the invitation of local industrialists, political figures, and other notables. As in his London lectures, he strongly expressed ideas that the more privileged classes found uncomfortable—ideas that in time would form part of the foundations of the United Kingdom's Labor Party as well as those of other political and social organizations. Most viewers of Garibaldi's brig expected, or at least hoped, that he would address the public at large while he was in the North East. After three weeks at anchor, however, he felt obliged to report that he had been "called home," and sailed back to Italy. But that did not end the North East's association with him.

At or around the point of Garibaldi's departure for Italy in April 1854, the Organized People of Tyneside, including local groups such as the Friends of European Freedom, gathered at Newcastle upon Tyne and there presented to Garibaldi a gold-hilted sword and a periscope as tokens of their esteem.

Homer's association with this celebrated figure was quite different. In the autumn of 1860, *Harper's Weekly* had asked him to prepare a portrait drawing of Garibaldi in military uniform set within decorative detail, some of which would pertain to Garibaldi's leadership. Whether this detail was left to Homer entirely is unknown but Homer was certainly capable of it all. The drawing was to be the basis of a full-page wood engraving printed on the front page of the *Weekly* for November 17, 1860.

Homer based his portrait of Garibaldi on a professional photograph of a bust portrait of the subject painted earlier in 1860 by the Italian artist Eleuterio Pagliano. As Garibaldi had resided on Staten Island in 1850, the *Weekly* had reason to devote its front-page illustration to a person who was not only an international military hero but also, in his way, a New Yorker. For more than a century this quite impressive wood-engraved illustration was unrecorded as a work by Homer.[6]

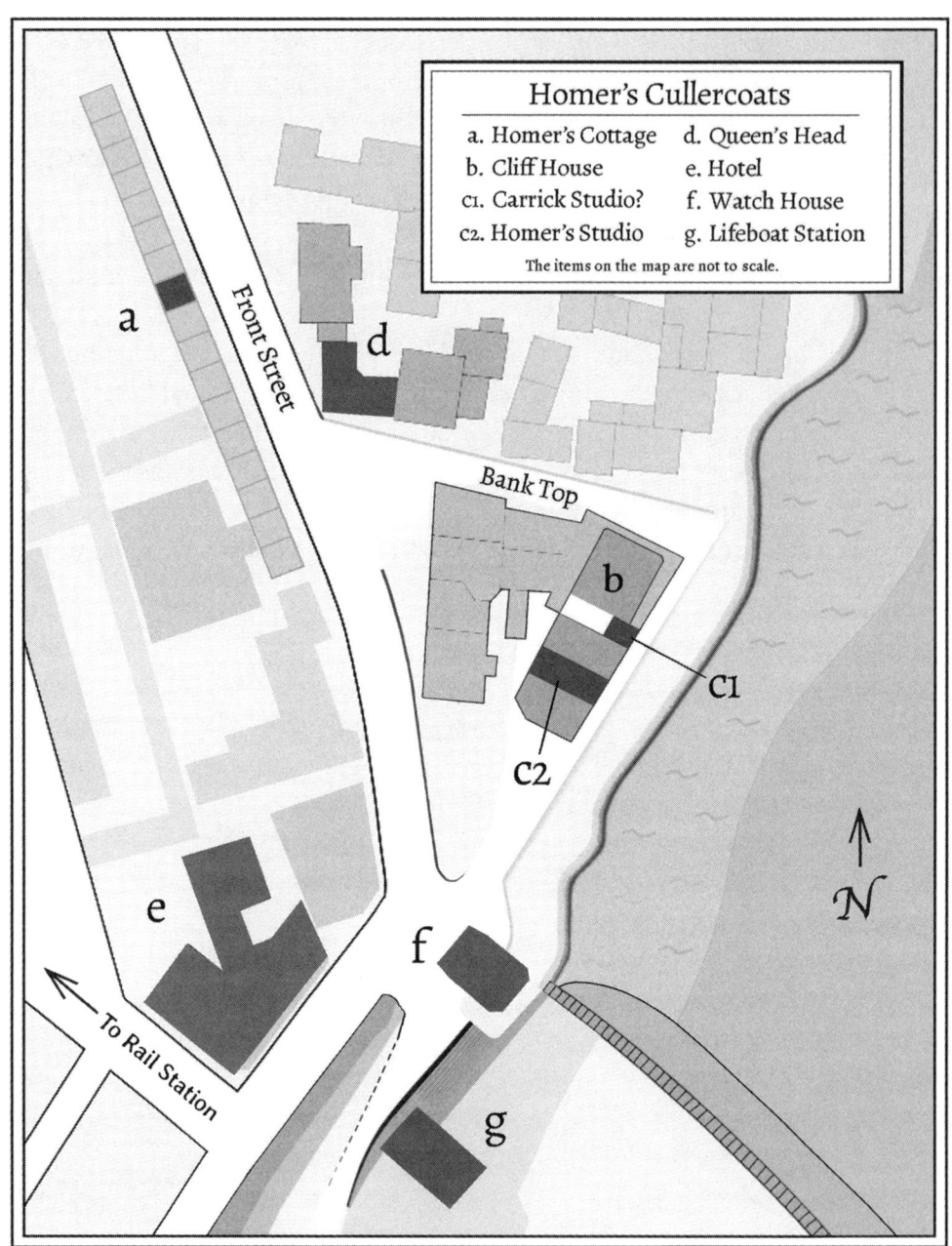

Map 1. Homer's Cullercoats. Legacy Graphics.

4

Homer's Cullercoats

THE VILLAGE OF CULLERCOATS as Homer knew it was neither spacious nor quaint. It occupied merely fifteen acres, and its character had little in common with the conventional English country villages of literature appearing in works ranging from Jane Austen to Agatha Christie. During Homer's residence, Cullercoats was administratively part of the much larger and infinitely more fashionable town of Tynemouth, located along the coast just to the south.

Cullercoats' chief feature was its great bay. The village stood on elevations of land overlooking this body of water. Homer occasionally made use of the bay in his paintings, though he did so in such varied ways that one may peruse his Cullercoats paintings without seeming to return to a familiar view. The layout of the village itself remains evident today, though lacking most of the buildings Homer knew. The meeting of two key streets along the edge of the bay, Front and Victoria Crescent, forms a north–south thoroughfare. Front Street ran to the north and was lined with attached cottages. Homer resided in one of these cottages that had been vacated by a fisherman prior to the artist's arrival (the cottage is described in more detail later in this chapter). Homer established his studio a few minutes' walk from his cottage. The much longer Victoria Crescent ran south to Tynemouth. Its Cullercoats end held a row of upscale terraced residences facing the bay. Homer's middle-class friends the Adamsons resided on Victoria Crescent.

At the meeting of Front Street and Victoria Crescent stood the village Watch House, known more formally as the Cullercoats Life Brigade Watch House. This was a weather-resistant station for volunteer observers who scoured the waters of the bay and the sea beyond it for vessels or individuals in distress. It had opened two years prior to Homer's arrival. The connection of Front Street and Victoria Crescent that passed the Watch House served in a sense as a boundary. On one side sat the village proper where life involved many small things. On the other side sat the bay where life centered on one big thing, the sea. Homer brought both sides into his Cullercoats work.

Across from the Watch House in what amounted to the heart of the village stood a handsomely designed three-story hotel, the Huddleston Arms. Homer had resided there for a week or two following his April arrival in the village.[1] Within a short walk from the hotel were several shops including those of picture-framers as well as three public houses (pubs). Somewhat further on, beginning in mid-1882, stood the village rail station, which replaced the one that for a decade and a half had stood well south of the village center.

From February to August the village fishermen sailed as a fleet of dark-sailed cobles to their fishing grounds well off the coast. For the autumn season, they shifted to waters closer to the bay. The fishwives prepared the cobles for sailing, baited fishing lines, sold the catch, prepared the cobles for their next sailing, and raised families. Many of the fisherfolk had descended from the small group of coastal fishermen who in the 1740s had settled at this site by invitation from the owner of the mostly unoccupied land by the bay. By the 1880s this fisherfolk-founded village had become a pleasant and busy suburb within the metropolitan area surrounding the flourishing historic city of Newcastle upon Tyne. Newcastle was one of England's larger cities, prosperous and advanced in its civic culture.

The Cullercoats fishermen beached their flat-bottomed cobles on the sands by the bay. Except in uncommon high tides, the bay's floor gave more or less solid footing to the fishwives when they loaded and unloaded the cobles. The bay had no quay, but the long North Pier, built of stone and commonly called "The Breakwater," served several purposes including that of picking up or setting down passengers from cobles or dories.

Two buildings marked the village's official relationship with the bay. The Watch House offered visitors grand views of this body of water and its bordering heights. The building's clock, bell tower, and curving veranda appear in Homer's works. Its bell signaled both safety and alarm. A brief ringing announced the safe return to the village of the fishermen's fleet. An extended rapid ringing signaled a boat or person in distress and alerted the crew of the village's Royal National Lifeboat as well as the rest of the community to the emergency.

On the sands below the Front Street level was the Royal National Lifeboat Institute's Cullercoats Station. Built in 1848, the station's tall, wide door opening allowed rapid passage onto the sands of the Cullercoats lifeboat and its crew. The boat measured thirty-three feet in length, with a beam of eight to accommodate two rows of paired oarsmen. The Duke of Northumberland, Algernon George Percy, had funded both the station building and the lifeboat. At its launching, the lifeboat received the name "Percy."[2] In his paintings Homer at times reduced the size of the lifeboat to accommodate the needs of his composition. He did the same with the village's many cobles.

He included the Watch House prominently in *Watching the Tempest* (Plate 10) and also parts of it as details in other paintings and drawings. He made use of the tall, wide door opening of the Lifeboat Station as a setting for the standing figures of a few of the boat's crew in his unfinished oil painting *The Life Brigade.*

Of quite a different scale from these village structures was Homer's compact residence at 44B Front Street. This was one of two attached cottages that shared a small enclosed patio.[3] His stay at the hotel may have corresponded to the time required to refurbish his cottage's interior. He would have needed not only a few basic furnishings but also secure storage spaces for the safekeeping of steadily growing groups of drawings and watercolors. He may have arranged to rent this facility before arriving in the village, even while still in New York. Within a short walk of the cottage stood the Queen's Head, a pub popular with fishermen.

At some point, also early in his time in Cullercoats, Homer established his studio on Bank Top, a relatively short street running off Front. The studio's precise location has in recent years become a somewhat unsettled matter. In this regard it has not helped that all but one of the residential buildings Homer would have known on Bank Top were pulled down in or around 1929. The exception, farthest along the street, was the quite substantial Cliff House. Built in 1768 as a private residence, it remains so as an English Heritage Grade II Listed Building of architectural significance. The house's stables, which Homer would have known, were taken down early in the twentieth century with the arrival of motor vehicles.

The location of Homer's studio is an important matter, for he must have spent a great deal of time working in it. He undoubtedly made preliminary sketches and studies for many of his paintings at sites in and around the village and elsewhere, but he would most often have executed the watercolors themselves in his studio.

Since the 1890s, published accounts of Homer in Cullercoats have claimed with certainty that his studio occupied a second-level south-facing room of no great size at No. 12 Bank Top, a building housing several residents. There has always been reason to question this claim, for Homer's art making in Culler-coats almost certainly required more space and better light.

No. 12 Bank Top, flanked by Nos. 11 and 13, were gabled multiple residential buildings. Homer sketched a semblance of this row as seen from the bay level in his charcoal drawing of 1882, *Men Beaching a Boat* (Plate 1). In it, a group of fishermen push and heave to beach a coble. The boat has been fitted for this effort with beaching wheels (aka launching wheels).[4] Homer's depiction of these buildings above the cliff-like bankside is a free generalization of what existed. Of less height to the right is Homer's suggestion of Cliff House.

The belief that Homer's studio occupied a south-facing room on the second level of No. 12 has its source in a book published in 1893, a dozen years after Homer had left the village. This was William Weaver Tomlinson's *Historical Notes on Cullercoats, Whitley, and Monkseaton*. Tomlinson, who had never met Homer, was then engaged in writing the history of the North East Rail Company, a study based on extensive and meticulous documentation.[5] He found time also to write Northumberland-based travel books for general readers. In these he used a more informal literary style as well as a casual approach to documentation that at times consisted of little more than hearsay. In his *Historical Notes* Tomlinson states, "Winslow Homer while at Cullercoats used as a studio a room in the house (12 Bank Top) occupied by a Miss [Jane] Carrick, the daughter of Thomas Carrick, who for his skill as a miniature painter and his invention of painting his portraits on marble instead of ivory, gained a considerable reputation during the earlier part of the Victorian era."[6]

Tomlinson leaves an impression that No. 12 was nothing more than Jane Carrick's home, though it was in fact a multiple-occupancy building. There is also reason to think that during Homer's time in the village Jane Carrick did not reside in No. 12 but lived elsewhere in Cullercoats.[7]

After retiring from a long and successful career in London, Thomas Carrick had moved to Cullercoats to be near his daughter. While in London he had earned a national reputation as an artist of note, mostly as a portraitist but also as a painter of English landscapes. His many London sitters had included such eminent figures as Thomas Carlyle, Eliza Cook, Henry Wadsworth Longfellow, Sir Robert Peel, and William Wordsworth. He had received a medal from Prince Albert in 1845 and a Turner Annuity from the Royal Academy in 1867. It seems unlikely that Carrick would have trooped such Northumbrian sitters as he may have had up the stairs of a building that housed several families and led them into a small south-facing room that had been pressed into service as a studio.

In his discussion of the site of Homer's workplace, the Cullercoats local historian Lloyd Reed has proposed that Thomas Carrick had indeed maintained a studio on Bank Top, and that it was a ground-level, single-story, purpose-built, north-facing structure of modest size. What he describes would have accommodated a painter of portraits, a sitter, and the artist's equipage. Reed believes that Carrick had erected this structure in the space now informally called "the gap" that separated the gable end of No. 13 Bank Top from Cliff House. He states that the studio had a multipaned north-facing window and perhaps a skylight as well. A tall wall running along the street from No. 13 to the grounds of Cliff House kept the studio building out of public view.[8] One hopes that photographic evidence of this structure will someday reach publication.

During Homer's time in the village he came to know at least a few local residents of significant social standing. The best documented of these was William Adamson (1815–1892), a solicitor based in Newcastle. He resided with his wife Hannah and their children in Garden House on Victoria Crescent. Their handsome building with its pediment-graced classical revival entry offered a panoramic view of the bay.

Adamson and Homer had much in common. The solicitor was a skillful amateur painter in watercolors, taking as his subjects coastal landscapes and local architecture of interest. Both men knew much about military matters. Homer had gained his knowledge firsthand as an observer during the American Civil War, making drawings at the front as a Special Artist for *Harper's Weekly*. Adamson had served a decade earlier during the Crimean War as an officer in the Northumberland Volunteer Militia, holding rank as Senior Captain and later as Honorary Major. He compiled and edited the volume *Notices of the Services of the 27th Northumberland Light Infantry Militia*.[9]

As both a solicitor and a private member of the community, Adamson had accomplished much for the public good in Newcastle, Tynemouth, and Cullercoats. In Newcastle, he was a benefactor of several cultural organizations including that city's Literary and Philosophical Society.[10] In Cullercoats Adamson was a helpful friend to the fisherfolk community, arranging benefits for its members in times of distress or disaster.

Adamson also served the Royal National Lifeboat Institute in several roles. A pleasantly journalistic report of the launching of a new lifeboat at Tynemouth mentions his presence in an official role, accompanied by two most distinguished companions. The account gives even greater attention to Adamson's wife, Hannah. Something of this happy event survives in an undated description of the launch.

> The new lifeboat was launched with an unusual degree of ceremony. The boat is 33 feet long and 8 feet wide . . . and is a specimen of a British lifeboat thoroughly equipped for service. The weather being very fine, a large crowd assembled on [Tynemouth's] North Pier and around the Prior's Haven [a small beach], which was gaily decorated with flags. The boat, which is large and handsome in appearance, was mounted on its carriage awaiting the moment when it should be launched . . . while on either side were gathered the crew, a sturdy company of men clad in cork jackets.
>
> About two o'clock Lord Ravensworth accompanied by the venerable Archdeacon Bland and William Adamson, Esq., Honorary Secretary of the Newcastle and Tynemouth branch of the National Lifeboat Institute, arrived at the spot, the band to greet them, having played the "National Anthem." After the Archdeacon's prayer, Mrs. William Adamson stepped forward to the bow of the boat from whence was suspended a bottle of wine. Swinging this smartly against the side of the noble little vessel, she broke it, and as its contents fell upon the boat said, "I name this boat the 'Constance,' may God speed it." In a moment the vessel flew down to the water's edge amid cheers of the assembled multitude and the stirring strains of *Rule Britannia*. (Constance was also the name of the Adamsons' eldest daughter.)[11]

The five Adamson children in order of birth were Bryan, Constance, Alan, Elinor, and Augusta Ann. Of these Alan is best known in the Homer literature as the Adamson son who, not having succeeded in his attempts to begin an engineering career in England, elected to seek opportunities in a different field in the United States. Perhaps at the senior Adamson's request, or at least with his consent, Homer wrote a brief letter of introduction and recommendation for Alan, stating that the young man "visits America for the purpose of farming." Homer addressed the note to a well-connected friend, A. Warren Kelsey in New York, concluding it with the conventional "consider any favor done for Mr. Adamson as done for me." In America Alan Adamson in time settled in Kansas, became a successful farmer, and purchased a Kansas newspaper, the *Beloit Daily Call*. He spent the following decades as its publisher and editor.[12]

In 1922, retired but still alert to national news, Alan Adamson saw a report that the Worcester (Massachusetts) Art Museum had acquired Homer's Cullercoats-based oil painting *The Gale* for an amount far surpassing anything

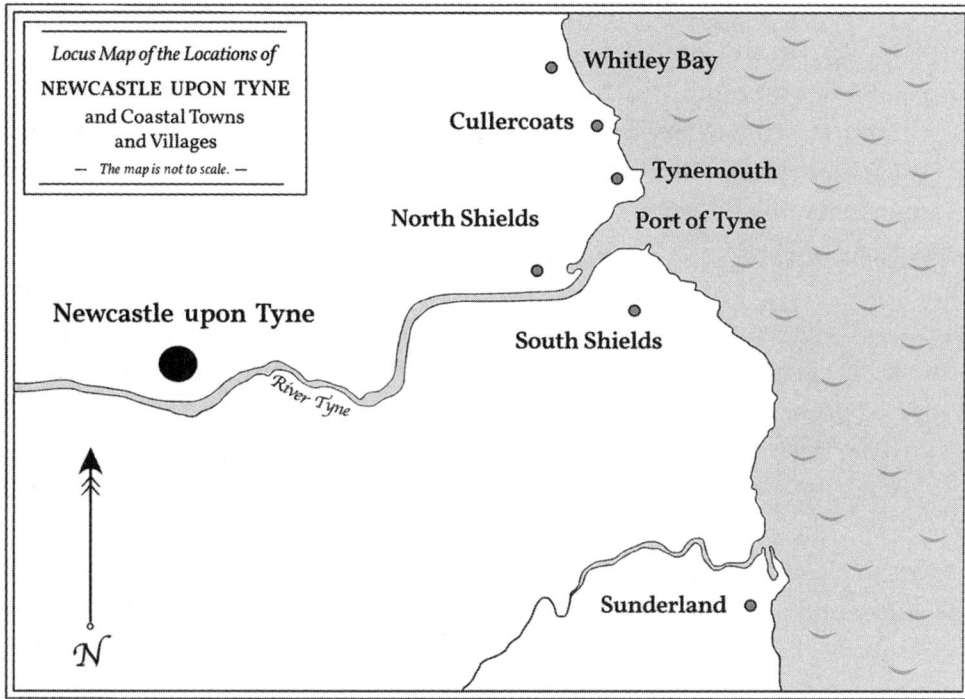

Map 2. Locus Map of Newcastle upon Tyne. Legacy Graphics.

known to have been paid previously for an American painting. This inspired Adamson to write a memoir of his acquaintanceship with Homer forty-two years earlier. His unpublished manuscript, found in family papers late in the twentieth century, first reached publication in 1988 in the catalogue for the exhibition *Winslow Homer, All the Cullercoats Paintings*. The full text also appeared in 2004 in Tony Harrison's *Winslow Homer in England*.[13]

As the River Tyne approached Tynemouth it broadened to meet the sea. Within this breadth was the international Port of Tyne with its docks, quays, warehouses, factories, and other buildings set into the banks and the land behind them. It was one of England's busiest ports as well as one of its most historic. The Romans had established a fortified settlement here, Arbeia, with an accompanying port. They put the port to use heavily during the construction, staffing, and maintenance of Hadrian's Wall.

The Port of Tyne made possible the successes of Newcastle's thriving shipbuilding, ship repair, heavy armament, and other industries. Ships arrived at the port with cargoes and passengers from around the world. Many left with cargoes of goods manufactured in the region, but often the outward-bound cargo consisted of "coals from Newcastle." For many decades coal shipped from Newcastle had heated London and other major communities both in England and across the North Sea.

Since the early 1870s Cullercoats had each summer enjoyed a slight but temporary swelling of its population when several visiting artists, professionals and amateurs alike, settled in for the season. They joined artists who were permanent residents of the village to constitute the Cullercoats Art Colony. Only a few of the colony's members were or became figures of national reputation, but the work of the others has contributed to the documentation of a historically significant fishing community in the years just before and after it reached a point of decline.[14]

Homer succeeded better than anyone in the art colony in pictorializing the essence of the fisherfolk both as individuals and as a community. He did this even while giving almost no pictorial attention to the men of the community or to the many older fishwives. Other members of the art colony, such as the able Robert Jobling (1841–1923), at times offered interesting alternatives to Homer's characterizations of the fisherfolk. Yet it is Homer's work that invariably appears to be more insightful and intimate in feeling than the work of the others. Homer offered a broader and more knowing comprehension of the community, one amounting almost to a feeling of affiliation.

A few accounts of Homer in Cullercoats note that some members of the art colony found him to be aloof, as indeed had some of his American colleagues over the years. In these characterizations he was not unfriendly so much as distant. Indeed, from early in his career Homer had been naturally a person of great reserve. By the 1880s he had become an artist of high rank, having been elected early in his career to full membership in the National Academy of Design, the American equivalent of the United Kingdom's Royal Academy. Though never a braggart, his quiet reserve could sometimes be taken as a stance of superiority. Honors aside, no member of the Cullercoats Art Colony accomplished so much as Homer did in bringing the village to life pictorially. This was little known or understood at the time, for in Cullercoats he had exhibited scarcely any of his paintings.

Though always well mannered, Homer was neither clubbable nor a seeker of solitude. In Cullercoats he became something of a workaholic, seemingly devoting most of his waking hours to painting and drawing. This was not altogether unusual for him, but as had been the case in America, it left him seeming to be unsociable.

5

Fishwives

Watching from the Cliffs, 1881. Watercolor. Reynolda House Museum of American Art, Winston-Salem, North Carolina. G&G 1028. (Plate 2)

Four Fishwives, 1881. Watercolor. Ruth Chandler Williamson Gallery, Scripps College, Claremont, California. G&G 1060. (Plate 3)

Homecoming, 1883. Watercolor. Arkell Art Museum, Canajoharie, New York. G&G 1178. (Plate 4)

THIS CHAPTER begins an examination of a selection of Homer's more ambitious and highly finished Cullercoats watercolors, a discussion that will continue throughout the following chapters 6, 7, 8, and 9. Homer's practice of dating each work with only the year of its making leaves the group with no sequential order. Most of the paintings are products of 1881 or 1882, though a few reached completion in 1883 and Homer dated them accordingly. He gave no significant attention to the seasons in this body of work; for instance, there are no winter snow scenes.

These Cullercoats watercolors are more complex in their subjects and design than most of Homer's smaller Cullercoats paintings, of which there are many. Few of the smaller watercolors reflect aspects of the adventurous manner so prominent in what he had recently painted in Gloucester, Massachusetts, during the summer of 1880 when his plans for England were most likely well advanced.[1] Both groups of watercolors, those from Gloucester and those from Cullercoats, stand as important but distinctly different bodies of Homer's most important midcareer work.

He began to paint in Cullercoats perhaps as early as late April 1881. His early paintings showed a revived interest in figural work, one that centered on groupings of Cullercoats fisherfolk. His previous interest in depicting groups included major paintings of African American life in postemancipation

Virginia, such as his *Dressing for the Carnival*, 1877 (Metropolitan Museum of Art). Homer continued to sharpen his skills of observation in Cullercoats, bringing them steadily and vigorously to a level at least as high as that of his recent American work. These Cullercoats paintings have received relatively little close attention in the Homer literature.

The first evidence of Homer's English work came to the attention of the American audience early in 1882 when two of his paintings of Cullercoats fishwives reached exhibition in New York. They appeared in the American Watercolor Society's annual members' exhibition. The very subject of fishwives was new to many American observers.

In Victorian England the term "fishwife," as descended from its Old English origins, meant "fisherwoman" rather than "wife of a fisherman." A fishwife might be a widow or an unmarried woman. Homer set the fishwives not only on the bay's sands but also in boats near the coast as well as on cliffs and ledges along the village's heights and elsewhere. He often depicted fishwives engaged in some activity, even if only conversing with a fellow fishwife or waiting and watching for the village's fleet of cobles to return. His fishwives differed in almost every respect from his 1860s and 1870s images of American women as farmers' wives, country schoolteachers, milkmaids, ladies on beaches, and shepherdesses. The differences reflected not only dissimilarities of local cultures but also the newness of American life when compared to England's centuries of tradition.

He painted only the younger fishwives, those in their twenties or thirties, as well as a few teenaged fisherlasses. An appearance of youthfulness fit the active pictorial roles he had in mind for his models. It would also please his dealers, for images of bright young women did well in the American art market. No information survives concerning how many fishwives posed for him, but it could not have been many. His talents for gently altering the likeness of a model's features in a painting to avoid unwanted identification allowed him to pose a single fishwife for more than one figure in a single painting.

He seldom painted the village fishermen other than as shadows or figures with features unseen.[2] For much of the year the men's nights on the sea led them upon their return to the village to sleep through the day. This left them little time to pose for Homer or even to become acquainted with him. Most of the fishermen probably thought it not quite fitting for a man to pose for an artist, other than when the painting was to be a portrait.

Fisherlasses were apprentices of a sort, older teenagers preparing to be fishwives. One Cullercoats fisherlass, Margaret (Maggie) Jefferson, became Homer's preferred model throughout his time in Cullercoats. She was also his neighbor in the village and acted as a source of useful information about the village. In 1881 when Homer first met her, Maggie was age sixteen or seventeen and a confident young woman. It would be excessive to suggest that Maggie Jefferson became Homer's close friend, for differences in age and class would have argued against such familiarity. Nonetheless the two worked closely together throughout Homer's time in the village, with Maggie, according to tradition, never hesitant to suggest to her employer how he might improve a pose. In a few paintings he left Maggie's likeness seemingly close to life, altering perhaps the color of her hair. One measure of their closeness comes from the belief that it was to Maggie that Homer first remarked, late in his stay in the village, that he had originally planned to spend only three months in Cullercoats but spent eighteen instead owing chiefly to his liking of the village and its people. Maggie might perhaps have added that it was also his satisfaction with what he was achieving in his Cullercoats paintings that encouraged him repeatedly to prolong his residency. Maggie Jefferson is better known in the Homer literature by the surname Storey, which she later gained through marriage.

Most fishwives while selling their share of the catch to established customers alerted other residents on nearby streets to their presence through a street call. Most sold their fish within a few miles of Cullercoats, but some traveled as far as Newcastle and its surrounding towns by rail.

The Cullercoats fishwives were noted for the meticulous cleanliness of their attire, their wicker creels (scrubbed daily), their cottages, and themselves. They were noted also for their quite direct manner of speaking and their humor.[3]

A few of the fishwives Homer may have painted had already acquired a basic knowledge of how to hold a pose. They had done so as much as a decade or two earlier by serving as models in fishwife attire for artists of the Cullercoats Art Colony. From all evidence the fishwives Homer painted found him as an artist to be a likable person. His paintings suggest that he returned the compliment.

Always a keen observer and recorder of women, Homer had rarely before invested them with such active lives as he did in Cullercoats. He depicts fishwives in motion while laboring outdoors and then still while conversing with each other. When he presents them in small groups, they convey a sense of companionship and steadfastness. Not since the shepherdesses of his Houghton Farm paintings of 1878 had he portrayed female figures with such a sense of feeling.

In *Watching from the Cliffs* Homer depicts a younger fishwife on a height who holds a small child in her arms. She stands silhouetted against the sky, looking past the viewer to the sea as she watches for the return of the village's cobles. Her husband will be on one of these vessels. The painting's fair weather precludes worry that a coble might have been lost. Some English painters of the time had made much of such melodramatic possibilities. They did so usually by portraying the wife, mother, and children of a fisherman waiting in a state of anxiety for a long-overdue coble.[4]

Homer places his fishwife on a strong diagonal line he has softened with a run of grass. He emphasizes both the woman's centrality and the presence of the child in her arms. Another child some years older sits on the grass nearby.

A second fishwife almost certainly observed Homer painting this scene. An unwritten rule of the fisherfolk community held that when a fishwife posed for an artist, another fishwife needed to be present. This was essentially for propriety's sake, and it was a common practice of many women's professions in Victorian England. It explains why Homer so often included pairs of fishwives in his Cullercoats works. He paid those who modeled a standard wage of a shilling a session.

Members of the Cullercoats Art Colony, professionals and amateurs alike, had begun to use fishwives as posed models in the 1860s. The fishwives' colorful summer attire and the availability of interesting natural backgrounds proved enticing to painters, though most of the colony's artists seemed to have tackled the subject only once or a very few times. So far as is known no professional artist other than Homer painted fishwives so regularly, either in groups or as individuals. Few if any other artists of the region posed fishwives in such a variety of locations as Homer did. It seems probable that no notable American artist of Homer's generation painted so many well-defined, clothed female figures in the course of a year and a half as Homer did while in Cullercoats.

The physical closeness of mother and child in this painting amounted to something new in Homer's work. He had painted many children in America, at times with adult figures nearby, but they do not touch and each seems preoccupied with his or her own thoughts. Here, mother and child have become one.[5]

The watercolor's somewhat muted hues reflect what Homer must have noted soon after arrival in Cullercoats. Owing to Northumberland's latitude, the color of the light was less intense than what he had known in America, its shadows less sharp. For Homer to have found the equivalent of the Cullercoats latitude in North America, he would have needed to travel to Canada, go on to the northernmost tip of Labrador, and then look farther northward to distant Arctic waters. He was not of course obliged to reproduce color as he observed it. In some of his Cullercoats paintings he found reason to work from a more brilliant palette.

The painting's foreground is as much a painterly essay in color as it is a freely recorded representation of this spot's rock, vegetation, and moisture. It serves as a contrast to the more sharply outlined figure above it. The cliff top was one of several along the coast, all varied in height and shape.

Homer produced a close variant of the painting in which he replaced the seated child with a pair of seated fishwives. This is his *Watching from the Cliffs* (1882, Carnegie Museum of Art, Pittsburgh). Its strong center of interest remains the standing fishwife with her closely held child and her quietly confident dignity. She looks straight ahead to the sea.

In the same year he produced a very different treatment of the subject of waiting and watching in his *A Fisherman's Family, or The Lookout* (Museum of Fine Arts, Boston). In this watercolor he presents in profile a standing fishwife with two children by her side, one an adolescent and the other much younger. He poses them on Table Rocks, a formation overlooking the North Sea just north of Cullercoats. Smoke emerges from the stacks of a ship across the way. The smoke, the grey sky, and the prominent brown-orange-grey surfaces of the rocks all show Homer's virtuosity in his uses of transparent watercolors. This work is a bolder painting than the Reynolda House Museum's *Watching*, but one less intimate in its mood.

Homer used outline extensively in painting his Cullercoats figures. He did so to define, consolidate, and reinforce what he had observed and sketched. He did this with great effect and without using decorative line as he had in such Houghton Farm drawings as *Shepherdesses Resting*, 1879.

In late 1881 Homer sent his large Cullercoats watercolor, *Four Fishwives*, to New York for inclusion in the American Watercolor Society's 1882 annual exhibition of its members' new work. He undoubtedly chose this painting to represent him owing to its extensive and original figure work, as well as for its setting, one that would be novel to most American viewers. He sent a second Cullercoats watercolor as well, *Mending the Nets* (1881, National Gallery of Art, Washington, DC). This was a more contemplative work showing two seated fishwives baiting hooks. The pair of large watercolors gave critics and others their first opportunity to assess what Homer had been painting in England.

He must have been greatly disappointed if not stunned to find that the art press reviewers almost to a person disliked both works. One observant critic praised the new strengths he had found in Homer's figure drawing, but even so followed his colleagues in finding the subject of *Four Fishwives* as well as Homer's presentation of it intrinsically objectionable. For Americans of cultivated taste in the 1880s these British working-class women, laboring with their very unladylike crooked elbows jutting out toward the viewer and their shamelessly exposed forearms, were not a fit subject for High Art. This would have been especially so when a vogue for the aesthetic was abroad and Victorian prudery commanded public taste. None of the reviewers warmed to the less controversial net-mending scene.

In *Four Fishwives* a fisherlass who totes a toddler on her back (probably a sibling) strides with the group to the site on the sands where the cobles they attend will soon be beached. When they reach their cobles, the three older women will sort fish, load their wicker creels, and set out for village streets and beyond. Because the fisherlass is in most respects a fishwife-in-training, the painting's title count of four makes sense. Maggie sometimes posed as multiple figures in a single painting, as she seems to have done in *Four Fishwives* where there are facial similarities linking all four figures.

The Jefferson family resided at No. 45 Front Street, close by Homer at No. 44B.[6] Maggie Jefferson's elder sister by two years, Isabella (Belle), apparently also modeled for Homer, though less frequently.[7]

While photographs of Maggie in midlife and later show her to be a brunette, Homer on at least three occasions painted her as a blonde with complexion to match. An artist may of course paint hair in such hues as will suit an occasion. Homer's three paintings of Maggie as a blonde increased her pictorial significance within groupings of other figures. In addition to her appearance in *Four Fishwives* she appears as a blonde also in *Beach Scene, Cullercoats* (Plate 6) and *Bridlington Quay* (Plate 13). Homer in all likelihood painted her often as a single brunette figure, regularly varying her facial features.

In each of his three paintings of Maggie as a blonde, Homer depicted her with a young child. Maggie Jefferson would have no children of her own until after her marriage. By then Homer was securely reestablished in America.

It seems likely that Homer was among the first, if not the very first, to paint a group of spirited British fishwives striding across the sands of Cullercoats Bay to begin their workday. Earlier English artists had tended to depict much less energetic fishwives, rarely in groups, typically in static poses. Homer gave his group of four a sense of organization, determination, and communal vitality, qualities quite absent from virtually all paintings of fishwives in Cullercoats other than his own. It must soon have become apparent to both his models and local artists that he had not come to the village to paint individual figures, but rather to paint communal activity.

His four fishwives wear their traditional summer working attire of a short jacket over a close blouse above a tucked long blue skirt of corded wool flannel. A white apron and a shawl that could cover the head completed the traditional costume. At least in its coloring, this garb seems to have been distinctive to the Cullercoats fishwives. Other fishwife communities in the North East wore something similar in practicality if not in details or colors (see Plate 13). Later studio portrait photographs of Cullercoats fishwives show that when not working they dressed in the fashions of the time for Englishwomen of the upper level of the working class.[8] The rapid yet businesslike movement Homer gives his four figures reinforces the reputation of fishwives as persons of strength and independence in their jobs and in community life as well.

The male figure at right, used by Homer as a balancing element in the composition, is more generalized than the women to avoid drawing attention from them. Though more fully realized than nearly all other men in his Cullercoats paintings, the figure remains an accessory to the main subject— the women and their work.

In the distance at right a group of cobles sailing home approaches the beach. To balance this detail Homer places on the horizon at left a large ship trailing grey smoke as it passes. This is a steam-powered fishing trawler. The first of its kind had appeared four years prior to Homer's arrival in Cullercoats.[9] It caused great concern among the fisherfolk, for the advent of industrialized fishing threatened the fishing community's very existence.

With his inclusion on the horizon of both cobles and a machinelike trawler, Homer quietly transformed the painting. It ceased to be a straightforward presentation of traditional fisherfolk morning activity and became instead a scene with a quietly ironic undercurrent. Homer's depiction of both traditional fisherfolk and a trawler announced that the decline of Cullercoats as a fishing village had begun. In England's North East where the Industrial Revolution had so successfully established itself decades earlier, there could now be little doubt that mechanized fishing would someday be the rule.

Before Homer painted this scene, members of the Cullercoats fisherfolk community had appealed to the administrative councils in both Tynemouth and Cullercoats for relief from the trawlers' intrusions into their traditional North Sea fishing waters.[10] These appeals brought little satisfaction. The

Cullercoats fishing community nonetheless managed to survive for another thirty-five years, though gradually diminishing in size. During World War I what little remained of the community revived briefly when the presence of torpedo-carrying German U-boats kept trawlers in port. A few individual cobles later plied the waters, but a large organized fleet of fishermen never again met fishwives on the sands. Homer on a few other occasions while in Cullercoats included a passing trawler on the horizon of a painting, perhaps to remind himself of the impact that these vessels had already made on the way of life he was painting.

In the work's mid-distance, a dark band of crowded figures consisting mostly of fishwives awaits the arriving cobles at water's edge. They mark the ever-shifting point where the sands end and the sea begins. The figures form an almost decorative band left open at center for the entry of the cobles. Beyond this band lies the open water of the North Sea.

In *Homecoming* Homer presents a solitary fisherman on his way home from a night on the fishing grounds. He walks quietly with his two small daughters who have come along the path to meet him. In *Watching from the Cliffs* Homer had depicted filial affection by means of a fishwife holding her small child closely. That detail was subsidiary however to the painting's main subject of waiting and watching. In contrast, *Homecoming* takes filial affection as its main subject, and it does so simply and touchingly. The fisherman holds the hand of one daughter while she holds her younger sister. In his free arm he carries a sack containing his coble gear. The painting presents a naturalistic image of the happy progress of a reunion several minutes after it had begun.

In the background two cobles race by as they approach the entrance to the bay. In good weather and other agreeable circumstances, home-stretch racing such as this offered fishermen last-minute relief from the slow routines of fishing at sea. The contrast of these high-sailed, fast-moving vessels with the slow but steady pace of the fisherman and his daughters enlivens the composition. The sails offer an upward lift to a setting otherwise flat in its surround of land, rock, and water. These horizontals speak perhaps of the solid safeness of home.

In setting his sole full-length detailed painting of a Cullercoats fisherman as part of a domestic scene, Homer broke from the neo-Romantic Victorian image of the English fisherman as a heroic figure in contest with the sea. The painter John Dawson Watson (1832–1892), who worked in Cullercoats, was noted for such melodramatic works. Homer's heroic figures in Cullercoats were instead his village fishwives, heroic in a very different sense but heroic nonetheless.

The 1883 date on this painting suggests that it was either an unfinished work that Homer brought to New York for completion, or one developed in New York from sketches and studies he had made in Cullercoats. His ordinary practice was to date a painting after he had completed his finishing touches.

Homer's paintings of fishwives marked a vast though short-lived change in his depictions of women. A measure of the differences comes from a comparison of what appears in his *Four Fishwives* with one of his most notable slightly earlier paintings of American female figures. This was his oil painting *Promenade on the Beach*, 1880 (Museum of Fine Arts, Springfield, Massachusetts). Here he placed two matronly figures in a large and quiet open space. The well-dressed figures pass a large body of water that seems almost unmoving. A distant boat in full sail appears to be stationary. The source of the very bright light that illuminates the two figures is left to the viewer's imagination. The two women's oddly combined shadow runs back to touch the water's edge.

These women are from a privileged nonlaboring class quite different from that of Homer's fishwives. Such a breadth of social contrast made Homer in the 1880s an all but unique figure among his era's American painters of women.

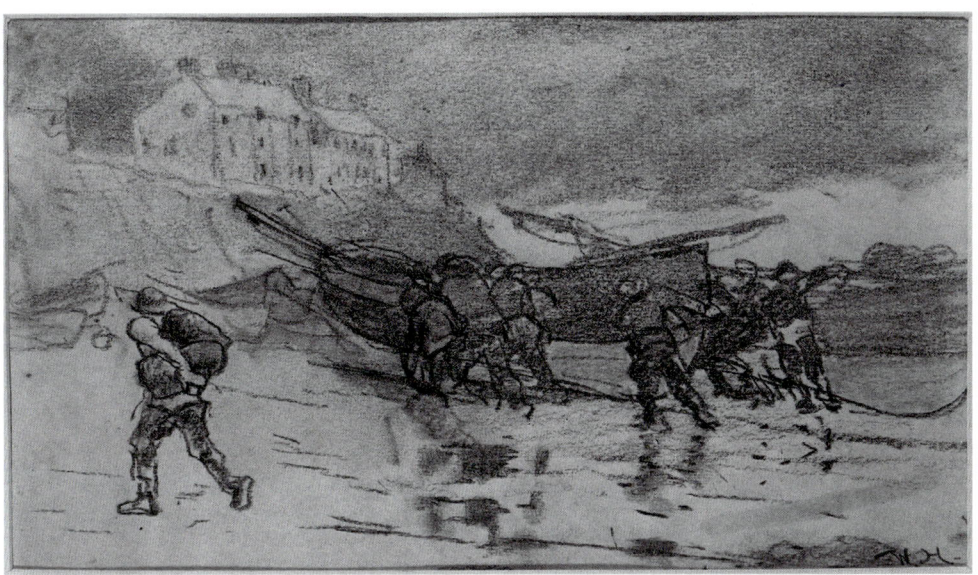

1. Winslow Homer, *Men Beaching a Boat*, 1881–1882. Black chalk on off-white wove paper, 17³⁄₁₆ × 12½ in. Harvard Art Museums/Fogg Museum, Cambridge, Massachusetts. Gift of Edward W. Forbes. 1953.202. Photo © President and Fellows of Harvard College.

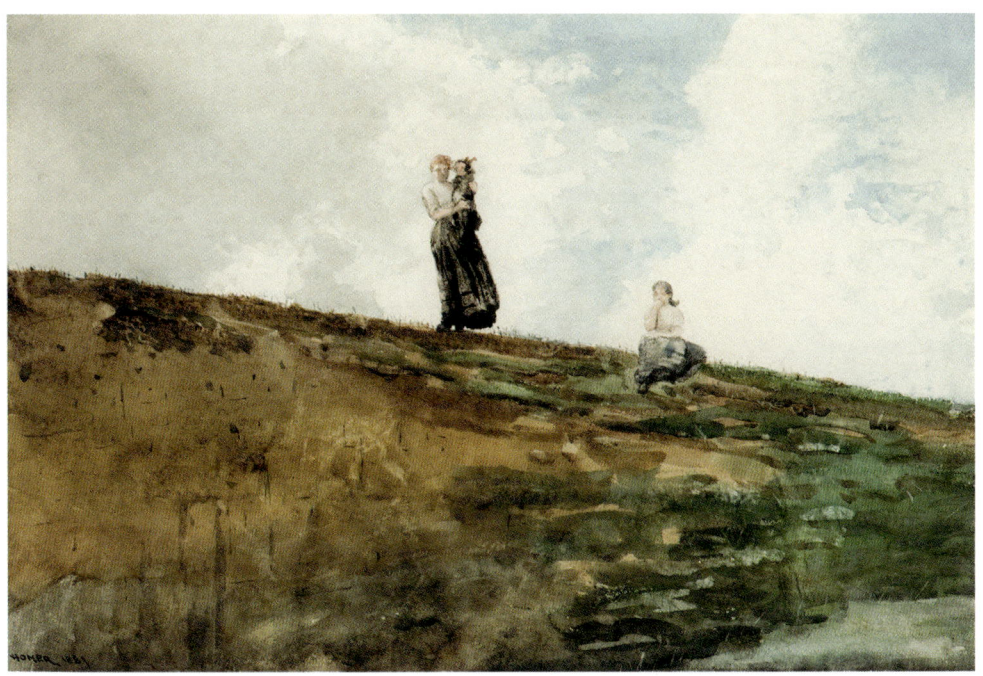

2. Winslow Homer, *Watching from the Cliffs*, 1881. Watercolor and graphite on medium-weight white watercolor paper, 13¹¹⁄₁₆ × 19½ in. Courtesy of Reynolda House Museum of American Art, affiliated with Wake Forest University, Winston-Salem, North Carolina. Bequest of Anne Cannon Reynolds Forsyth. 2003.2.1.

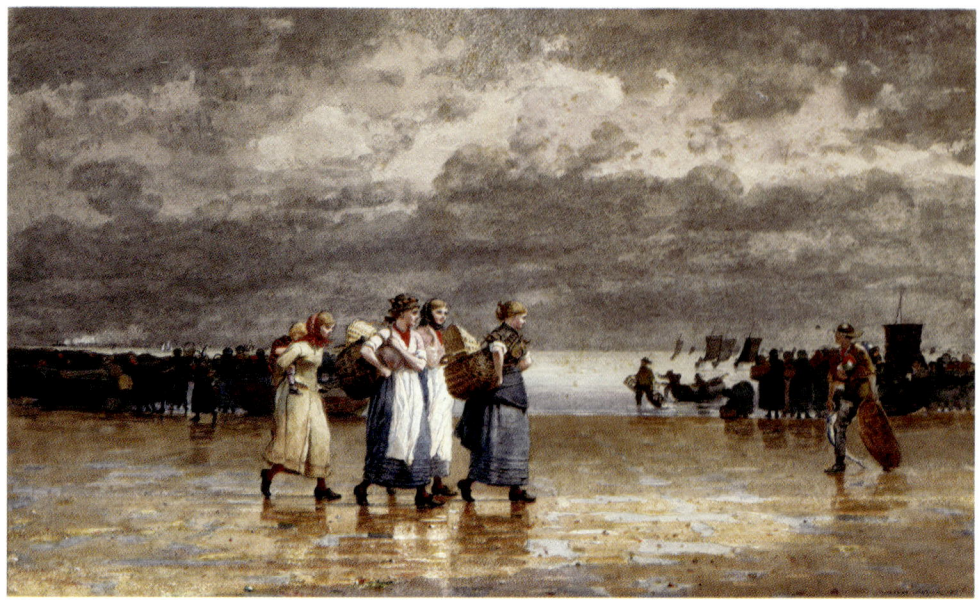

3. Winslow Homer, *Four Fishwives*, 1881. Watercolor on paper, 18 × 28 in. Ruth Chandler Williamson Gallery, Scripps College, Claremont, California. Gift of General and Mrs. Edward Clinton Young.

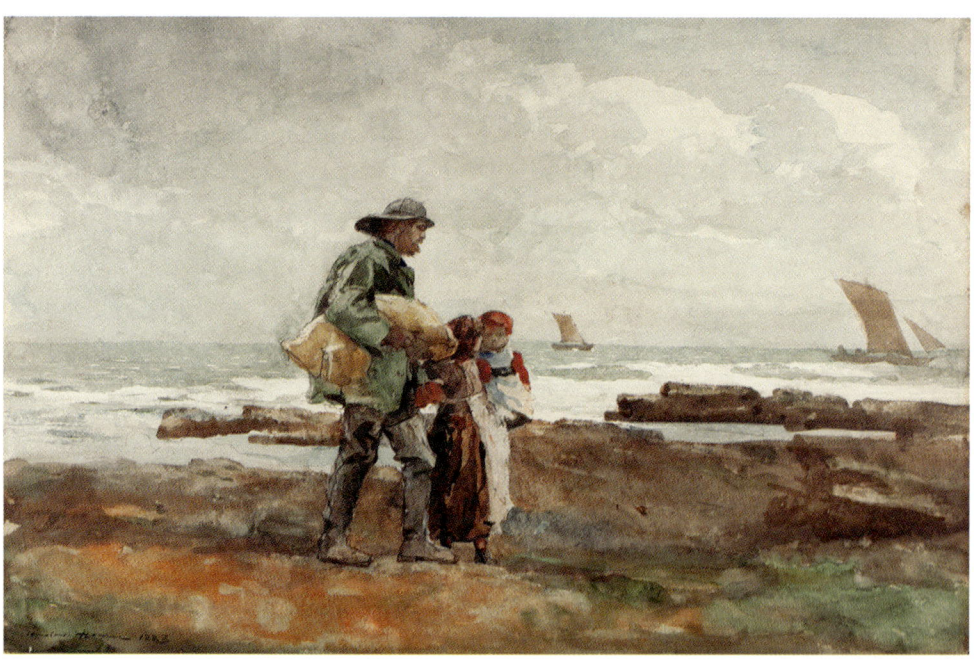

4. Winslow Homer (American, 1836–1910), *Homecoming*, 1883. Watercolor over graphite on wove paper, 14 7/16 x 21 ½ in. Collection of Arkell Museum, Canajoharie, New York, by bequest, 1946.

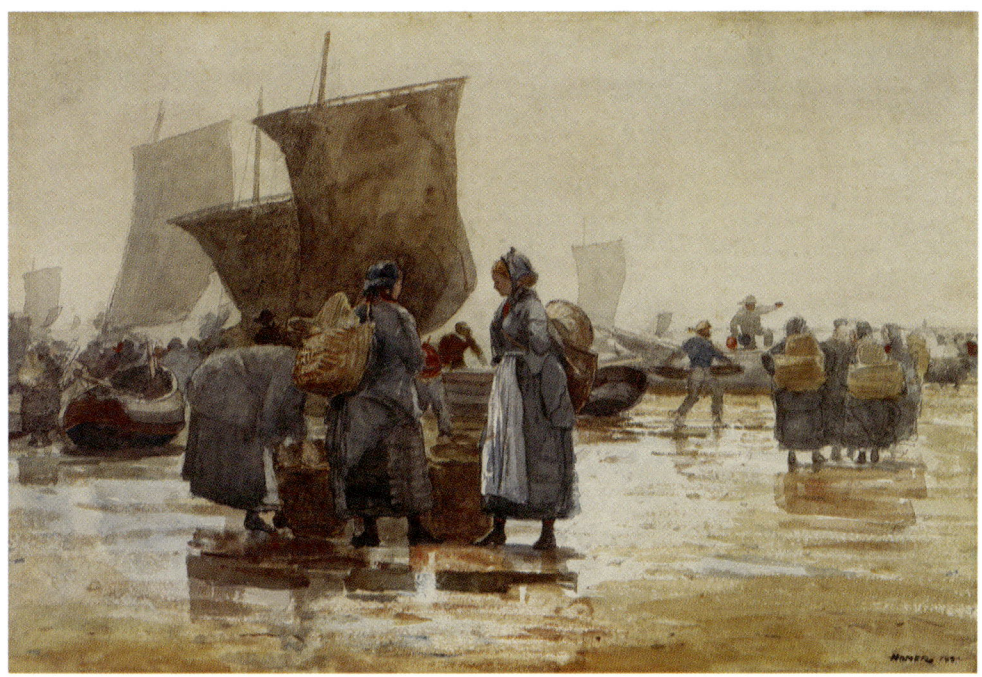

5. Winslow Homer, *Fisherfolk on the Beach at Cullercoats*, 1881. Watercolor, 13⁷/₁₆ × 19⁷/₁₆ in. Addison Gallery of American Art, Phillips Academy, Andover, Massachusetts. Gift of an anonymous donor. Bridgeman Images.

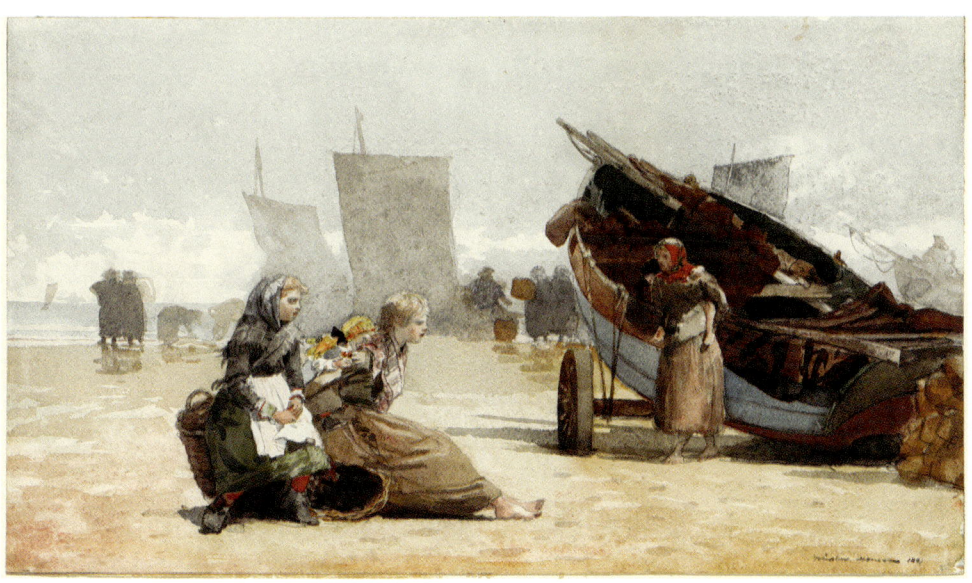

6. Winslow Homer, *Beach Scene, Cullercoats*, 1881. Watercolor over graphite on cream wove paper, 11⁷/₁₆ × 19½ in. Acquired by Sterling and Francine Clark, 1924. 1955.1490. Image courtesy of Clark Art Institute, Williamstown, Massachusetts, clarkart.edu.

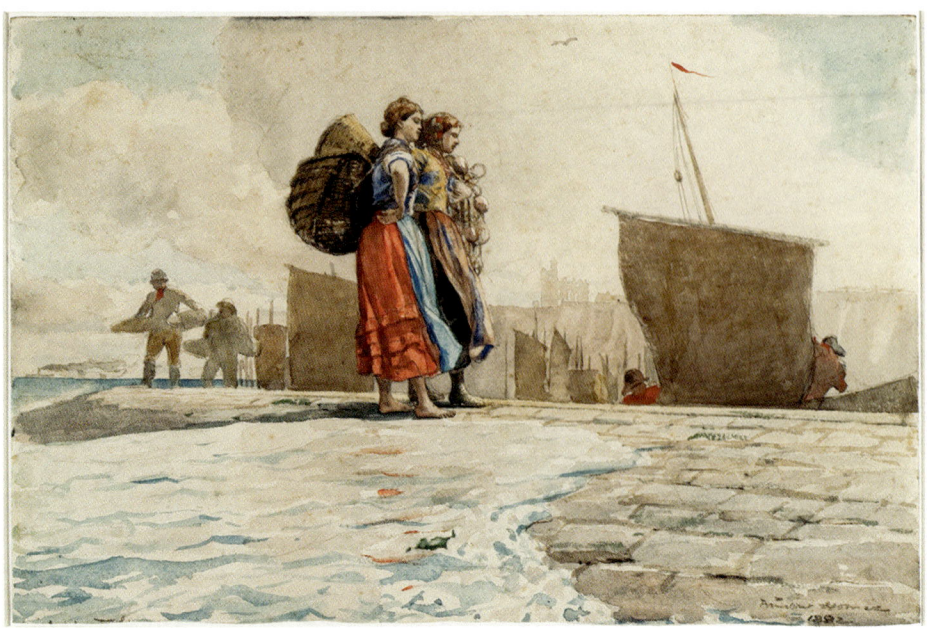

7. Winslow Homer (United States, 1836–1910), *The Breakwater, Cullercoats*, 1882. Transparent and opaque watercolor, over graphite, on ivory wove paper, 13¼ × 19¾ in. Portland Museum of Art, Portland, Maine. Bequest of Charles Shipman Payson. 1988.55.16. Image courtesy of Meyersphoto.com.

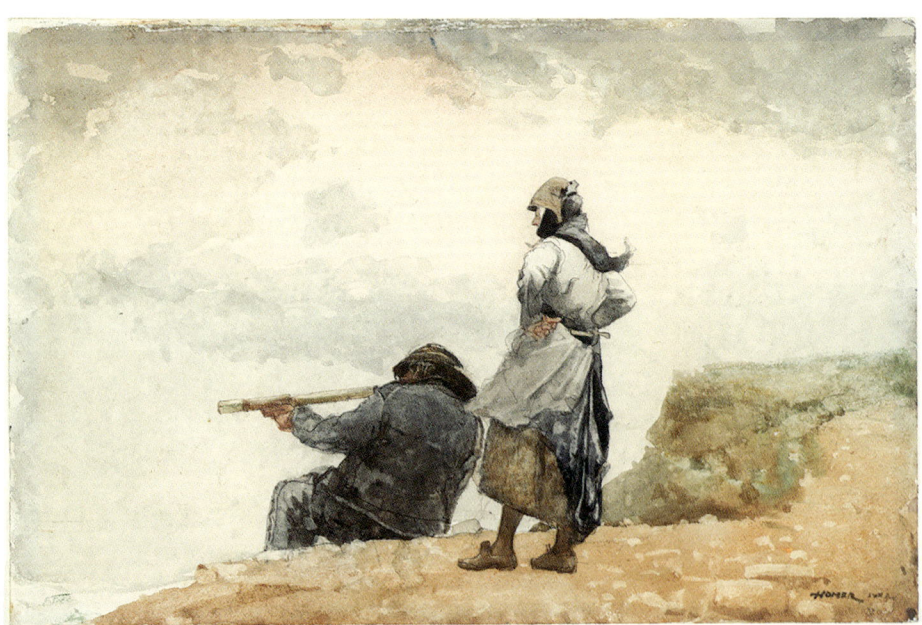

8. Winslow Homer, *The Lookout*, 1882. Watercolor over graphite on heavy white wove paper, 14⅝ × 21⅞ in. Harvard Art Museums/Fogg Museum, Cambridge, Massachusetts. Anonymous Gift. 1939.231. Photo © President and Fellows of Harvard College.

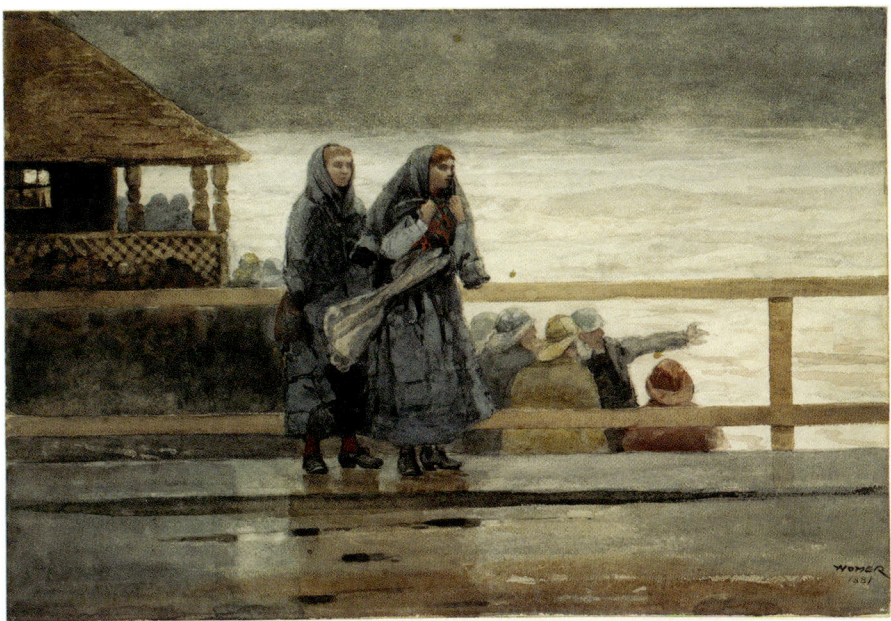

9. Winslow Homer, *Perils of the Sea*, 1881. Watercolor over graphite on cream wove paper, 14⅝ × 20¹⁵⁄₁₆ in. Acquired by Sterling and Francine Clark, 1927. 1955.774. Image courtesy of Clark Art Institute, Williamstown, Massachusetts, clarkart.edu.

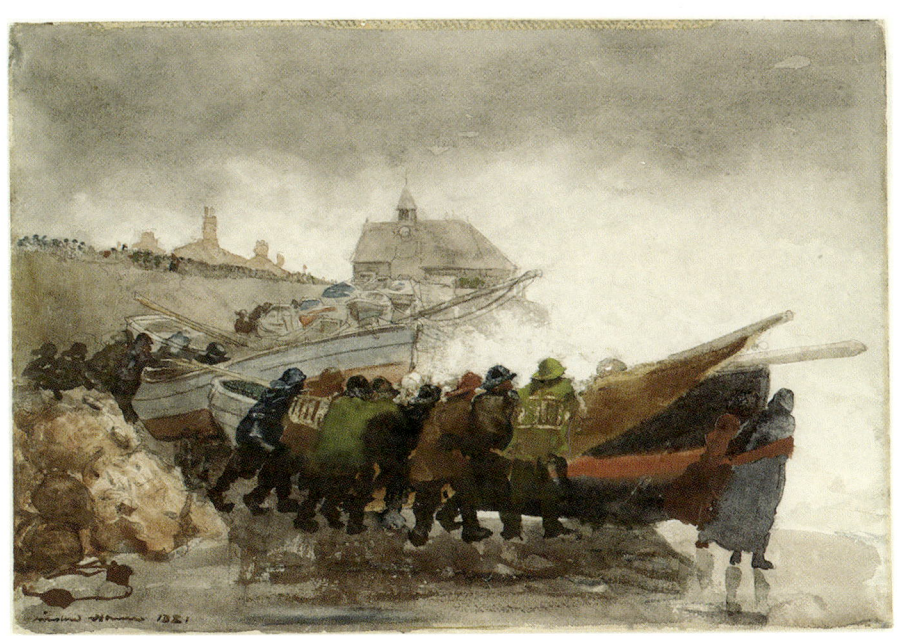

10. Winslow Homer, *Watching the Tempest*, 1881. Watercolor over graphite on off-white wove paper, 14 × 19¹³⁄₁₆ in. Harvard Art Museums/Fogg Museum, Cambridge, Massachusetts. Bequest of Grenville L. Winthrop. 1943.296. Photo © President and Fellows of Harvard College.

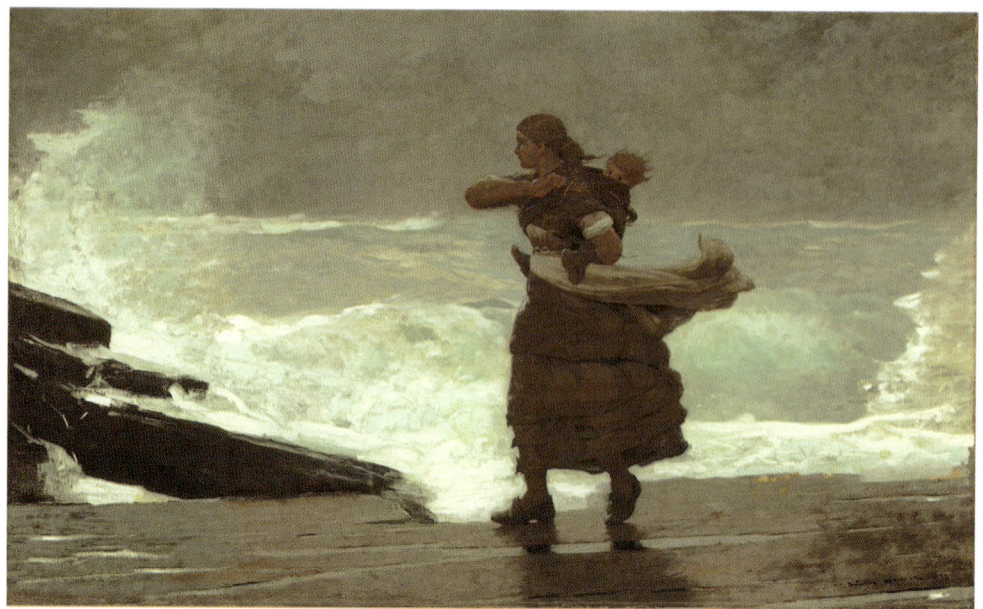

11. Winslow Homer, *The Gale*, 1883–1893. Oil on canvas, 30¼ × 48³⁄₁₆ in. Worcester Art Museum, Worcester, Massachusetts. Bridgeman Images.

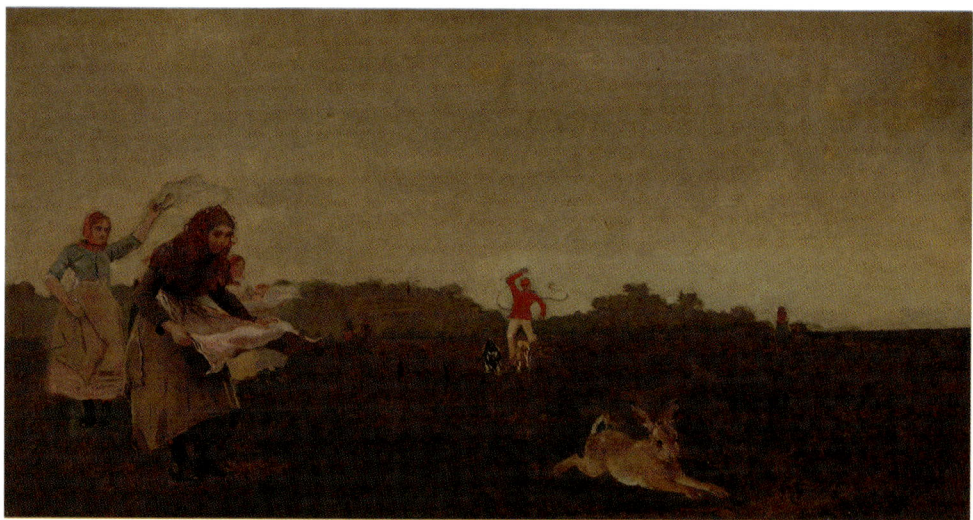

12. Winslow Homer (American, 1836–1910), *Coursing the Hare*, ca. 1882–1883. Oil on canvas, 14⅞ × 27½ in. (38 × 70 cm). Virginia Museum of Fine Arts, Richmond, Virginia. Paul Mellon Collection. Photography by Katherine Wetzel. © Virginia Museum of Fine Arts.

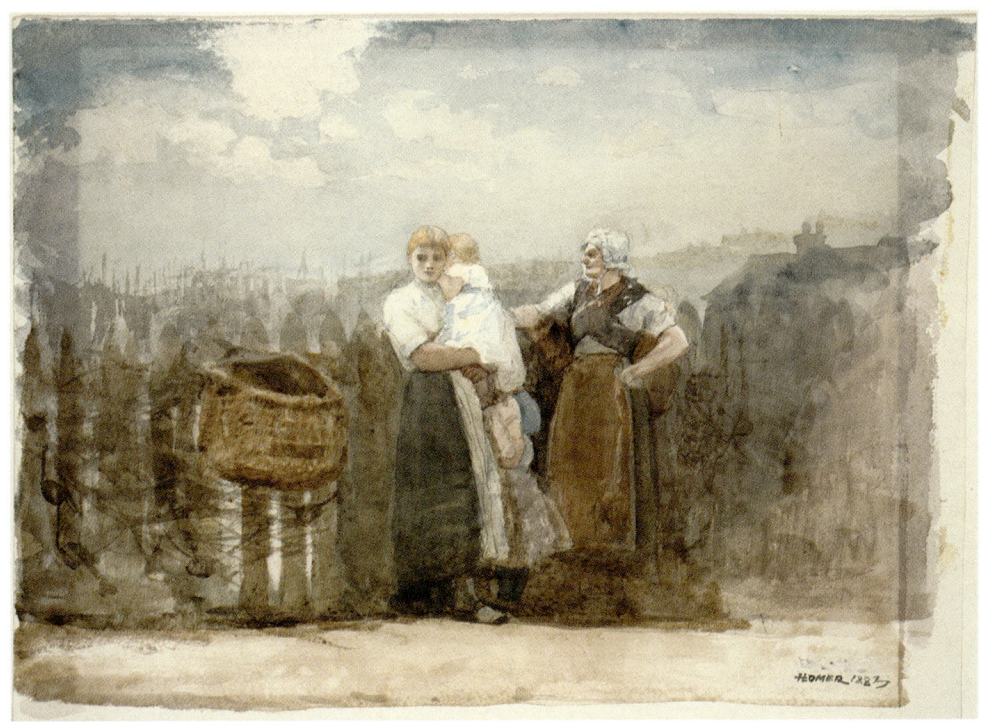

13. Winslow Homer (American, 1836–1910), *Bridlington Quay*, 1883. Watercolor over graphite pencil on paper, 13⅜ × 17¹³⁄₁₆ in. Museum of Fine Arts, Boston, Massachusetts. Bequest of Ralph W. Gray in memory of his father, Samuel S. Gray. 44.681. Photograph © 2021 Museum of Fine Arts, Boston.

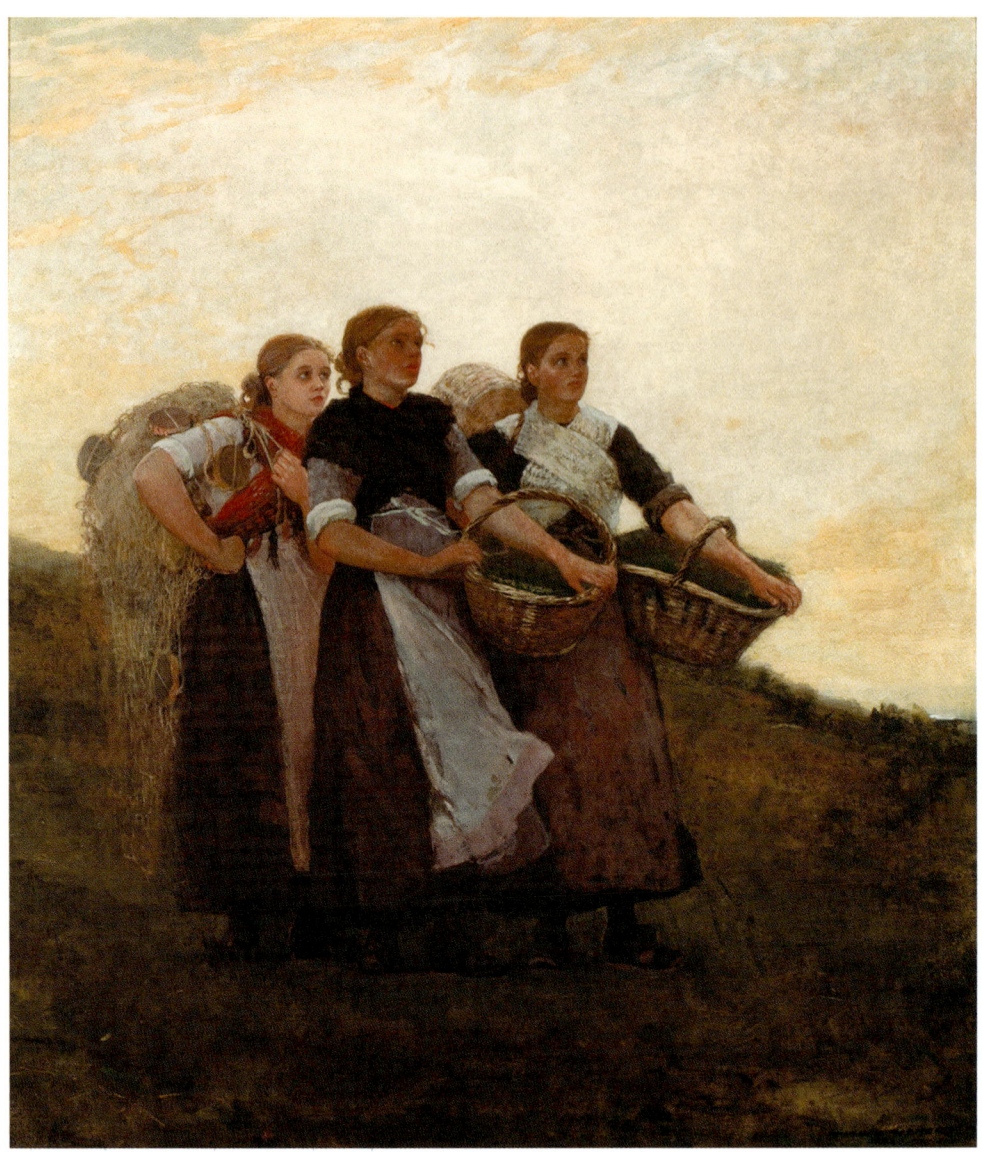

14. Winslow Homer (American, 1836–1910), *Hark! The Lark*, 1882. Oil on canvas, 36⅜ × 31⅜ in. (92.39 × 79.69 cm), framed: 48 × 43 × 4⅛ in. (121.92 × 109.22 × 10.48 cm). Layton Art Collection Inc., gift of Frederick Layton, at the Milwaukee Art Museum, Milwaukee, Wisconsin, L99. Photograph by John R. Glembin.

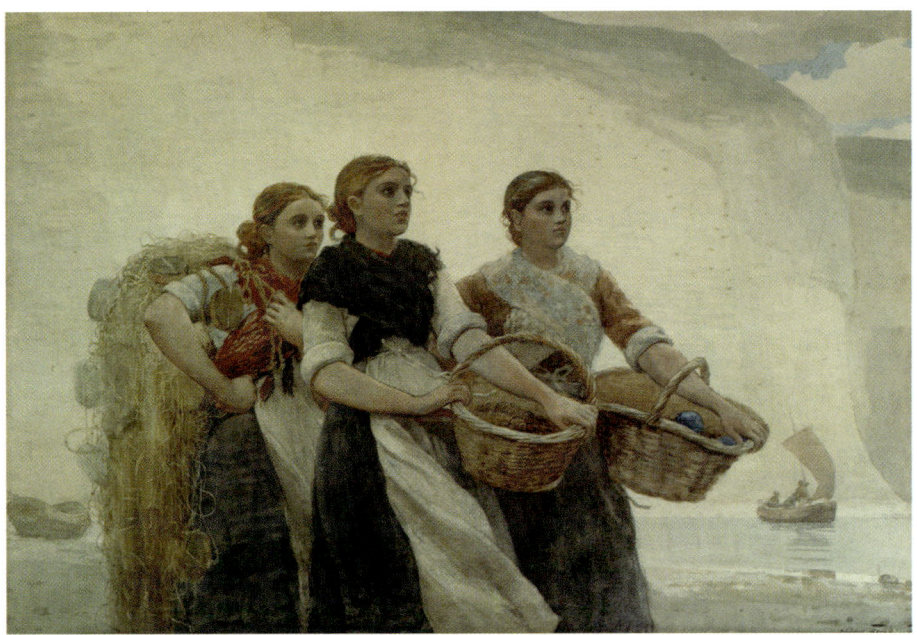

15. Winslow Homer, *A Voice from the Cliffs*, 1883. Watercolor, 21 × 30 in. Private Collection.

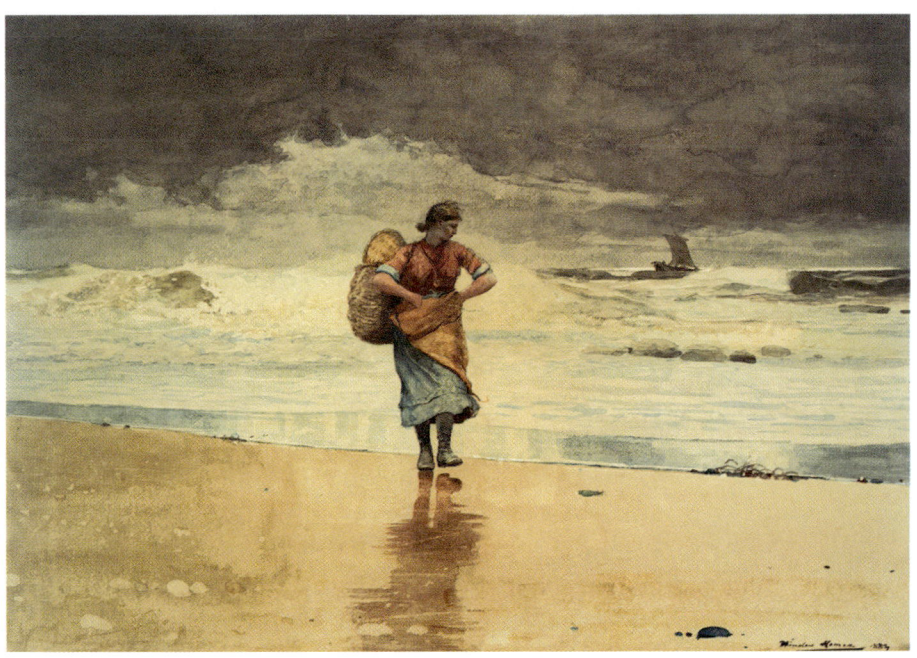

16. Winslow Homer, *The Incoming Tide*, 1883. Watercolor, 21½ × 29½ in. Printed with the permission of the American Academy of Arts and Letters, New York City, New York.

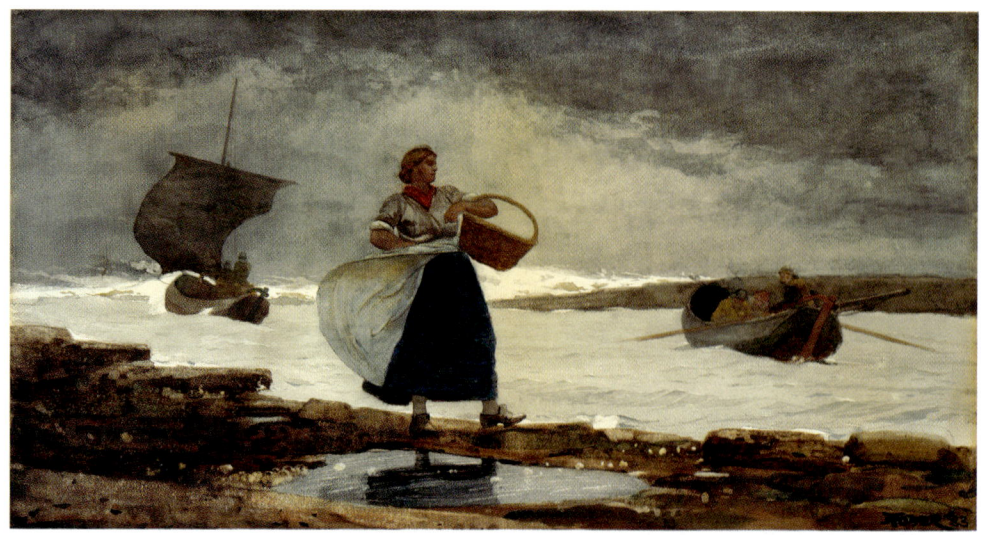

17. Winslow Homer, *Inside the Bar*, 1883. Watercolor and graphite on off-white wove paper, 16 × 29 in. The Metropolitan Museum of Art, New York City, New York, www.metmuseum.org. Gift of Louise Ryals Arkell, in memory of her husband, Bartlett Arkell, 1954. 54.183.

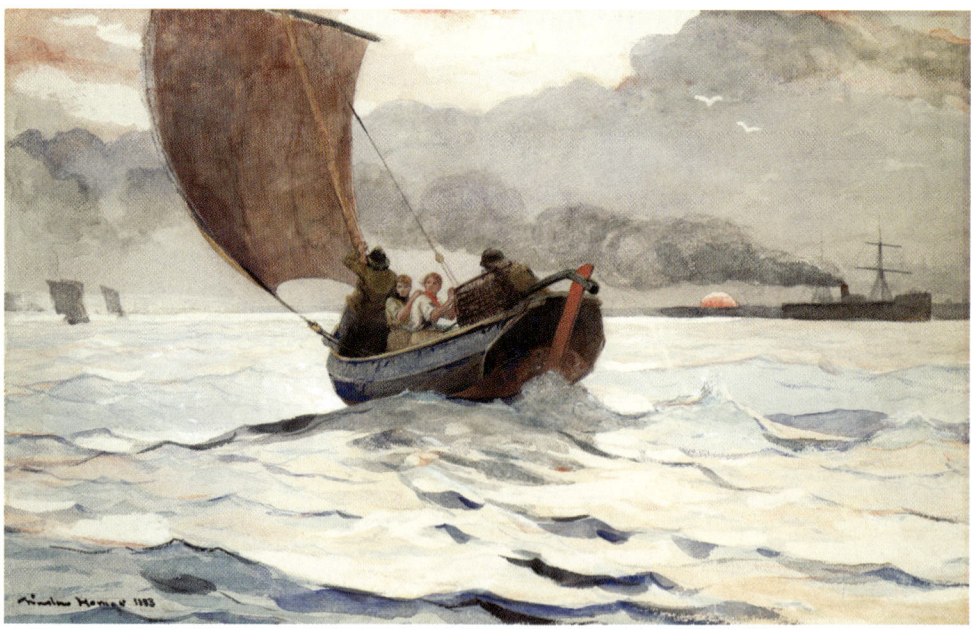

18. Winslow Homer, *Returning Fishing Boats*, 1883. Watercolor and white gouache over graphite on off-white wove paper, 16⅛ × 24¹⁵⁄₁₆ in. Harvard Art Museums/ Fogg Museum, Cambridge, Massachusetts. Anonymous Gift. 1939.233. Photo © President and Fellows of Harvard College.

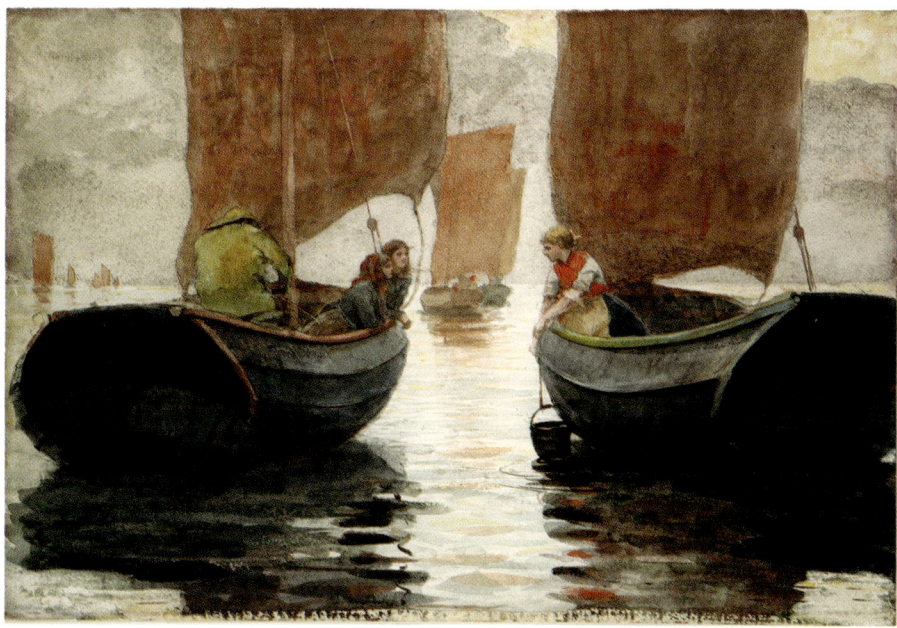

19. Winslow Homer (American, 1836–1910), *An Afterglow*, 1883. Water-color over graphite pencil on paper, 14¹⁵⁄₁₆ × 21⁹⁄₁₆ in. Museum of Fine Arts, Boston, Massachusetts. Bequest of William P. Blake in memory of his mother, Mary M. J. Dehon Blake. 22.606. Photograph © 2021 Museum of Fine Arts, Boston.

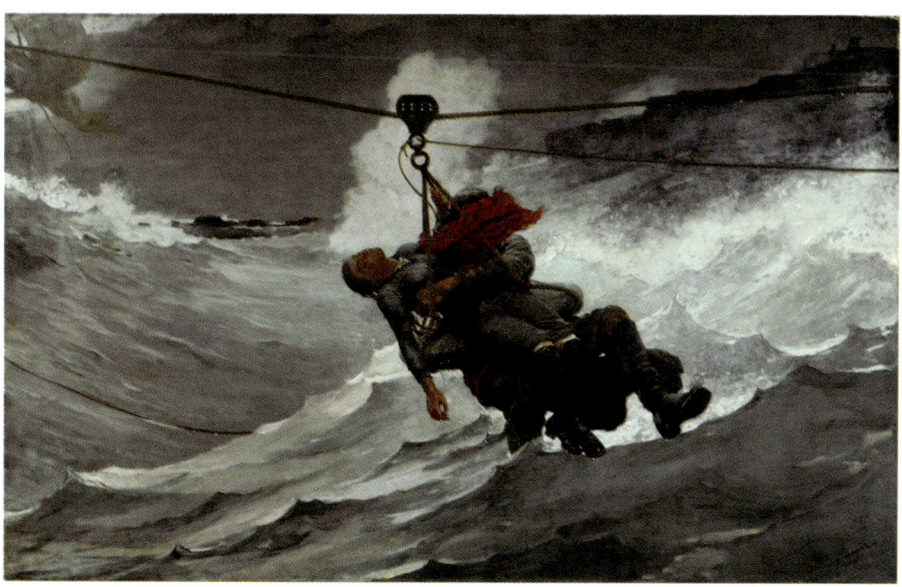

20. Winslow Homer, *The Life Line*, 1884. Oil on canvas, 28⅝ × 44¾ in. The George W. Elkins Collection, Philadelphia Museum of Art, Philadelphia, Pennsylvania. E1924-4-15.

6

On and above the Sands

Fisherfolk on the Beach at Cullercoats, 1881. Watercolor. Addison Gallery of American Art, Andover, Massachusetts. G&G 1050. (Plate 5)

Beach Scene, Cullercoats, 1881. Watercolor. Sterling and Francine Clark Art Institute, Williamstown, Massachusetts. G&G 1052. (Plate 6)

The Breakwater, Cullercoats, 1882. Watercolor. Portland Museum of Art, Portland, Maine. G&G 1114. (Plate 7)

The Lookout, 1882. Watercolor. Harvard Art Museums, Fogg Museum, Cambridge, Massachusetts. G&G 1130. (Plate 8)

FROM TIME TO TIME along the Northumberland coast, "Scotch mists" form when warm North Sea air rolls in over cooler land. The mists contain small droplets of moisture; larger droplets produce opaque fogs. Because the mists tend to rob a painter's subject of much of its clarity and color, they prove off-putting to many artists. Homer, however, took advantage of the Cullercoats mists, painting them both imaginatively and naturalistically as support for his narrative content. He contrasted light and heavy mists inventively. His artifice in this amounted to something new in his work, but it was a device to which he rarely returned once he had left Cullercoats.

In *Fisherfolk on the Beach*, one of his busier and more varied Cullercoats figural groups, he took as his subject some of the activity on the sands that followed the arrival and beaching of the fishing fleet. This brought the fisherfolk to a peak of community activity. The event gathered together fishermen, fishwives, children too young to be in school, villagers, and others. The fishermen, having often had little or no rest during their night at sea, attended directly to a set of long-established arrival tasks before heading home for a long day's sleep.

The tasks included the division of the boat's catch, which proceeded according to each crew member's seniority or share of ownership in the coble.

Most cobles had a crew of three. During this division, many fishwives filled their creels with layers of fish arranged for ease of individual extraction and then left for their routes. Fishwives not selling the catch remained on or near the sands to attend to such crucial tasks as baiting fishing lines and repairing tears in fishing nets. The cobles themselves underwent comprehensive cleaning. As an accompaniment to this activity across the sands there would have been sounds of voices talking, shouting, singing, and laughing. Homer here presents this ever-vital activity on a quiet misty morning.

Lloyd Goodrich, in his 1944 biography of Homer, might have had this or a similar Homer painting in mind when he observed of the Cullercoats fishwives that they were "sturdy, capable of men's work, ruddy from outdoor life, [and] handsome in their robust way." In comparing them to the female figures Homer had painted in America, Goodrich observed that the fishwives had a "new flexibility and motion, [and were] larger in form, rounder, more solid."[1]

In the foreground three fishwives pause in their labors to converse on the rain-soaked sands. In positioning the figures, Homer echoed the prominently slanted diagonal line of the tops of the two tall sails just behind them. He configures the fishwives on an axis that runs upward from the figure that stoops to the one who stands upright. He uses an angled creel to carry the line from one figure to the next. To the right, a single full-length standing fishwife brings a sense of order to the composition. Homer set these figures in a foreground that is somehow of a lighter mist than that in the pictorial space immediately behind it. The enveloping grey haze grows heavier as it recedes into the near distance, steadily lessening sharpness of details while also unifying the entire scene.

As contrast to these quietly standing fishwives, Homer places two active fishermen in the background's light mist. He positions both to reinforce the diagonal emphasis he has given to the fishwives and the sails. One fisherman with outstretched arms hurriedly carries a long object across the watery sands. The other fisherman stands in his dory with an arm outstretched, signaling or calling to others. In drawing these figures, quite likely from visual memory, Homer's quick execution adds a sense of life to the background.

As the mist grows heavier, it robs distant coble sails of their dark color. In the foreground its thinness allows the somewhat crisper detail of the three unmoving central figures to appear almost as a sculptural group. The dory at the left adds a further element of roundness. Homer's uses of the mists reinforces the fisherfolk's strong sense of unity, one gained through unremitting and self-directed community labor. The mist embraces it all.

Well before he undertook this watercolor, Homer had shown himself to be highly skilled in composing for the pictorial press outdoor groups of adults who shared common activities without losing their individuality. In the mid- to late 1850s he often depicted Bostonians shopping or otherwise engaged in busy outdoor settings. Among these wood-engraved images were his *View in Market Street, Boston*; *Emigrant Arrival at Constitution Wharf, Boston*; and *Family Playing Fox and Geese*, all dated 1857 and published in *Ballou's Pictorial Living Room Companion*, Boston.[2] These early graphic works are of course different in many respects from what Homer would do beginning in the 1860s as he turned his attention to painting. His skill in depicting groups of figures showed itself early.

Beach Scene, Cullercoats offers a very different composition and mood. In a first viewing, the work's sunny foreground with its three unusually posed figures seems to be from a wholly different world than that of the rest of the painting. In the near distance, a mist-shrouded group of fisherfolk attends to varied routine labors. Neither the three foreground figures nor those in the background show any awareness of the others. The foreground's three appear to be inert, though their poses and expressions quietly radiate life. The attention Homer gives them, as well as their provocative setting, encourages the viewer to cast about for a satisfactory reading of the entire image.

Might Homer here deal with memory, presenting the mist-enwrapped fisherfolk in the background as a remembered past? Or might the painting be concerned with the passage of time, for the sails of the middle ground's cobles rapidly lose what little remains of their color as they recede into background mist, as if slipping back in time. And for what purpose has he made the wrecked carcass of a coble the painting's major object?

The scene's two child minders, one seated and one standing, and the young fisherlass with folded hands who guards her empty creels, constitute the painting's major human elements. The three seem unrelated and hardly aware of each other or of the wreck. The seated barefoot fisherlass (posed by Maggie Jefferson) leans forward to adjust the weight of her toddler. There is little elegance in this or much sign of either affection or companionship. To the right the standing child minder, whose charge dangles a leg by her side, appears to be not only alone but also lonely. The downcast seated fisherlass with creels splays her feet in boredom. All three appear to be waiting, but for no visible reason.

As problematic as these figures may be, the object by which they rest is nothing less than a mystery. What can be said of this coble's massive weight, its bulk, the gathered wreckage it holds, or its heaven-angled prow? Where has it come from? Why has it been left so close to the water level? For what reason is it still equipped with the beaching wheels, which should have got it well up onto the sands to then be put to other uses? This puzzling foreground draws attention away from the mist-dimmed fisherfolk in the background, leaving them to perform their daily labors without an audience.

An unobtrusive but finely executed mist-bound detail just to the right of the wreck's stern shows a coble moving speedily ahead with a fisherman in its prow; he leans forward toward the bowsprit. The figure's scale, activity, and misted surroundings ally it to the painting's hazed fisherfolk of the background. He differs from them however in his vital presence, in the heaviness of his surrounding mist, and in his vessel's elevation well above the visible water level. How this detail might relate to the three foreground figures or the painting's setting remains a puzzle.

Despite the many questions Homer poses in *Beach Scene, Cullercoats*, its image remains among the most vivid and memorable of his Cullercoats paintings. The strikingly unconventional grouping of the fisherlasses and the two children act as an eye-catching centerpiece.

In *The Breakwater, Cullercoats*, Homer works from a low angle of vision, as if from a dory moored next to the Cullercoats Breakwater (also known as the North Pier). This long stone structure extending into Cullercoats Bay served among other functions as a site for the setting-down of passengers from dories, cobles, or other small vessels.

Homer's two young women stand quietly in bright sunlight as they look across the bay toward the village. One is a young fishwife attired in locally unconventional colors. The other is perhaps a visiting friend or relative. Unusually well groomed for her aquatic locale, this woman wears dress boots while the fishwife in red goes without footwear. She is an unusual image of a fishwife by Homer owing to the absence of any suggestion that she is actively engaged in fishwifely activities. She serves instead as an artful figure meant to provide a still and solid contrast to the actively moving figures who are emerging around her from nearby mists.

Just beyond the two women, a few Cullercoats fishermen who have returned to the bay begin the unloading of their cobles. The mist somehow remains absent from the breakwater itself. Homer contrasts the world of active labor with that of quiet contemplation, and sets obscurity against clarity and roughness against refinement. The women's naturalistic poses and colorful attire dominate the composition, but the mist-obscured laboring fishermen are more than staffage. Right of center one of them clambers up the far side of the breakwater, his coat somehow turned red as if absorbing the red-skirted fishwife's presence. Is this fanciful bit merely a product of Homer with a smile, playing fast and loose with academic naturalism? Nearby two fishermen carry loads to the breakwater while another takes down the sail of his coble.

The misty background includes the masts of more than a dozen vessels, some with their main sails still raised high. The masts of the more distant cobles carry the eye up the great cliffs of the neighboring Tynemouth head-land to the silhouetted ruins of the medieval priory and castle. These stand a hundred feet above sea level.

The ruins at Tynemouth attracted many tourists and more than a few art-ists. Once there the artists ordinarily approached and depicted this medieval site from viewpoints nearby. J. M. W. Turner, however, painted the striking assemblage from the sea and in doing so achieved highly dramatic images.[3] Homer himself traveled to the top of the headlands in 1882, but only to paint two presumably non-Cullercoats figures in his *The Lookout*. He did so without recording a view of the ruins.

In *The Breakwater* itself, masts right of center reinforce the upward thrust of the composition. The nontraditional colors of the fishwife's red corded skirt and blue apron may be a product of Homer's invention, but this figure's bare feet on sun-warmed stones surely reflects what he saw. The fishwife's two large empty creels may be for future use in an outward-bound coble. Homer catches the play of sunlight on the women's breeze-blown skirts giving a wel-come degree of movement to the scene. The breeze also moves the sail of the closest coble giving it for the moment a form in concert with the women's skirts. A mast-topping pennant confirms the breeze's strength.

The freshness of these two figures owes something to the watercolor medium Homer used so steadily in Cullercoats, as well as his brighter palette, but his sharpness of observation played a role as well. The figures' somewhat casual poses save them from being labeled "statuesque." One senses that to some degree Homer idealized the figures, but perhaps only to express his pleasure in the making of this work. On the horizon at left a fishing trawler passes.

Homer's *The Lookout* differs comprehensively from the paintings in which he made use of mists. Here he sets the scene in clear air atop Tynemouth's headland. He has included for atmospheric contrast a large white fog bank just offshore. The lookout sits securely on his makeshift seat as he concentrates on what he has spotted through his telescope. He has selected this location and undoubtedly returns to it with some regularity. He does so not because it presents a grand panorama of part of the North Sea but because it offers a view of the many ships that move by on their passage to or from the Port of Tyne. The port is to the lookout's right, well below him to the south.

The ships that most interested this observer were quite likely international vessels. They would have been varied in type, size, color, speed, and, most importantly, the flags that identified their nationalities. The lookout presumably has made a pastime of identifying each ship and speculating on its relationship to weather, international events, competition among shipping lines, and anything else that might concern the flow of traffic in and out of this very active port. He may have done so as a scout for a local shipping line or perhaps merely to entertain himself.

The lookout is not a Cullercoats fisherman, though he might once have been one. If his companion—spouse, daughter, friend—is a fishwife, she is not from Cullercoats, for her attire lacks the obligatory color, cording, and trimness distinctive to the village. She is in some ways the antithesis of the two standing figures in *The Breakwater*.

It is possible that a Cullercoats fishwife posed for this figure in a Homer-approved, tossed-together costume, yet there is nothing here of the poise typical of Homer's Cullercoats fishwives. The lookout's companion stands with hands on her hips in a relaxed pose, with weight on her right foot, presumably waiting for the lookout to conclude his sightings and accompany her away from his perch-on-high. A strong breeze tugs at her apron and raises a corner of her shawl, telling her to move along with her companion. The contrast of the lookout's companion with Homer's fishwife in red on the breakwater requires no mist to show them to be from two rather different worlds. That Homer brought such fine draughtsmanship to this well-composed rendering of the lookout and his somewhat disheveled companion indicates how seriously he took the subject. There is nothing of caricature in this work, though perhaps a smidgeon of good humor.

He may have arranged for transport to the top of this headland for himself and his sketching paraphernalia, but a simpler way would have been to travel by NER from the Cullercoats station to that of Tynemouth—the next stop on the line. He may of course have been taken there by acquaintances.

7

Storm

Perils of the Sea, 1881. Watercolor. Sterling and Francine Clark Art Institute, Williamstown, Massachusetts. G&G 1094. (Plate 9)

Watching the Tempest, 1881. Watercolor. Harvard Art Museums, Fogg Museum, Cambridge, Massachusetts. G&G 1084. (Plate 10)

The Gale, 1883–1893. Oil on canvas. Worcester Art Museum, Worcester, Massachusetts. G&G 1511. (Plate 11)

A MARINE STORM as an entity in itself, consisting of wind, rain, lightning, and a high sea, rarely held interest for Homer as a painter. He preferred instead to examine human behavior in relation to the prospect of a storm or its aftermath. While in Cullercoats, he twice took as a subject the responses of fisherfolk to a worrisome or even dangerous storm, but in so doing he kept the storm itself offstage. A third storm subject, quite late in his association with the village, proved to be something very different, calling on much invention and taking a decade to reach a lasting resolution of its parts.

Neither the village of Cullercoats nor the rest of the North East was a particularly stormy part of England. As noted earlier, that distinction belonged to England's South West, particularly Cornwall and Wales. In published discussions of the country's stormiest parts, the North East typically goes unmentioned.[1] Indeed, Cullercoats, Newcastle, and most of the rest of the region enjoyed a relatively pleasant climate. The protection of the Pennine Range to the west, and the relatively warm waters of the North Sea to the east, exerted a moderating influence on the coastal communities. Homer may have found December and January in Cullercoats to have been warmer and less snowy than those months he had known in Boston and New York.

Perils of the Sea, the quietest of Homer's storm-related paintings, presents two fishwives who stand alone by a handrail across from the veranda of the

Cullercoats Watch House. The fishwives have pulled up their shawls to warm their heads while they give their attention to something toward the south end of the flooded bay, which is not visible in the painting. The flooding of the bay has come from high tides occasioned by the passage of a heavy storm off the coast.

A group of men stand on a level below the walkway, each wearing a sou'wester. This collapsible oiled-fabric head covering had a back flap to protect its user's neck from sun and rain. In the nineteenth century sou'westers became a common article of workmen's wet-weather wear in England, the United States, and elsewhere. Homer found the shape and details of this head covering sufficiently interesting as elements of design that he later painted a row of sou'westers in use.[2]

One of the men below points with an outstretched arm in the direction that has drawn the women's attention. Figures on the adjacent Watch House veranda look instead out to sea. Nothing in the scene suggests a nearby oncoming storm or a danger of any sort. Perhaps the event at the south end of the bay is in the nature of a coble that has pulled its anchor and floats free. Because the Volunteer Life Brigade has apparently not launched its lifeboat, all seems safe. Though the painting's title speaks of "perils," none are apparent.

The painting's title may not have been chosen by Homer, for he often left that task to his dealers. Whoever named it borrowed the title from the then widely popular hymn of the same name.[3]

While *Perils* lacks the drama of violent weather, it nonetheless depicts flooding brought about by a North Sea storm. The floodwaters have covered the sands deeply enough to enable waves spawned at sea to roll into Cullercoats Bay. Homer's articulation of the moving surfaces of the flooded bay is effective in its subtle ranges of whiteness and in the contours and rhythms of its lateral lines. Mists and a darkened sky remove all sight of the surrounding world, leaving Cullercoats and its bay alone and seemingly adrift on a sea of its own.

In the late 1880s, half a dozen years after his return from Cullercoats, Homer taught himself etching. He etched his plates in his Prout's Neck studio and then sent them to New York to be printed in what proved to be small editions by a professional etching printer.[4] He adapted three of the subjects from his Cullercoats watercolors, altering details and otherwise refining his designs.

One of the three watercolors was *Perils of the Sea*. For the etching Homer eliminated the handrail, and this alone made the two fishwives seem more imperiled. He also did away with the outstretched arm of the male figure on the lower level as well as the silhouetted figures on the Watch House veranda. These changes tightened the composition. Adjustments of tonality in the etching had a similar unifying effect. Lost were the subtleties of the painting's colors, the blues and the tans, but gained was a sharpened, still quietly anxious mood.

In *Watching the Tempest*, a much busier composition for a more complex subject, something of great import is occurring in or on the flooded Cullercoats Bay, but it is not visible in the painting. Homer does not identify what is happening but instead depicts the anxiety and curiosity of the crowded onlookers as with great intensity they watch an unfolding event. A small wave that has just crashed against the sea wall behind the foreground figures fills the air with a shower of spray. This was a storm-born wave's last act after traveling from the sea onto and across Cullercoats Bay. The responses of the foreground figures range from alarm to enthrallment. In this respect especially, *Watching the Tempest* is a very different work from *Perils*.

Watching's title suggests that the onlookers are studying the storm, but they may also be observing something occurring within it. Might the Life Brigade be at work at the other end of the bay? Might the storm be wreaking havoc among beached cobles? Homer includes no such detail of narrative but establishes a mood of communal anxiety with a tightly constructed overall design of sharp-edged angles, unrelieved diagonals, and heavy crowding. He intensifies what he has shown in the foreground with adjacent rows of tightly packed boats that ascend the steep slope that leads upward to the village level and safety.

The foreground figures lean against a coble for protection from wind and spray. Some hold tightly to the coble's gunwales. At the end of this row of figures a fishwife chances the elements as she bends and turns to peer around the coble's bow. Homer configures the boat's bowsprit and folded sail to suggest what might be taken as the maw of a marauding sea beast.

At lower left a large outcropping of stone helps to anchor the scene, but here too its surface is one of unsteady diagonals and sharp angles. Anticipation of the storm's possible fury keeps the foreground figures in apparent states of stress.

Relief arrives for the painting's viewer when nothing less than the village Watch House settles the scene. Homer presents it in full profile to cap and quiet the anxious activity. A symbol of order and safety with its solidly reassuring uprights and gracefully sloped roof line, the structure imposes a sense of stability on the composition.

To the left of the structure, in the background, gables and chimneys rise like Don Quixote's giants to peer over the surrounding line of figures who have come to watch the bay and its events from the village's street level. Homer calms this energetic construction with subdued color.

No endangered fisherfolk appear in either *Perils* or *Watching*. To have included such figures would have carried Homer into the world of pictorial fiction. He remained as he had always been, a painter of the world as he had observed it while perhaps also improving on what he had seen without altering its essential meanings. In his Cullercoats paintings he included nothing so patently dramatic as the colossal breakers that pound against cliffs in his oils of the 1890s and later. Indeed, his Cullercoats watercolors offered not much more in the way of a violent sea than the hearty collision at the painting's sea wall of a bathing beach–scale wave reaching the end of its journey.

Because gales are storms of strongly sustained winds of high velocity, but little if any rain, it is tempting to think of them as somehow simpler and less damaging than marine storms. Yet gale winds can approach hurricane force. Toward the close of his time in Cullercoats, Homer chose to paint in oils a young Cullercoats fishwife who crosses a dock while struggling against a gale. She seeks safety on shore not only for herself but even more so for the young son she totes on her back. The subject added to the multiple strengths Homer had already conferred on Cullercoats fishwives in earlier paintings. His use of the oil paint medium was surely a measure of the importance of this work in his thinking.

In this new and much larger than usual work, which he titled *The Coming Away of the Gale*, Homer marked his return to New York. In doing so he chose to include content that distinguished the painting from his recently much praised 1883 Cullercoats watercolors. It did so, but in ways that proved to be conceptually confusing to critics and others. Thus the painting made a shambles of what could have been Homer's celebratory return to the New York art world.[5]

When the National Academy presented *The Coming Away* in its annual members' exhibition in April 1883, two things were immediately apparent. The first was the size of the canvas. It measured some three by four and a half feet, very much larger than any other work Homer had painted in Cullercoats or shown in New York. The second thing quickly apparent was the highly unusual content of the left half of this oblong composition. Painted with great precision, and thus lacking strong painterly effect, Homer had set his fishwife adjacent to a coble with beaching wheels stationed close by the dock. Immediately beyond this coble, and seemingly within arm's reach of it, Homer carefully painted a close view of part of the veranda of the Cullercoats Watch House with its sloping roof. These two things—a wheeled boat and part of a lookout station—undoubtedly mystified or confused viewers.

Homer placed his image of the Cullercoats fishwife to the right of the painting's center with her son safely on her back. He depicted her moving forward against a strong wind toward safety on shore. She and her son constitute a strongly conceived and painted pair of figures, but it was the red-headed boy's features, though occupying much less of the canvas than his mother, that became a strongly appealing center of interest. From the start Homer seems to have wanted his painting to be not so much a summation of the great strengths of his Cullercoats fishwives, but rather something closer to his own farewell to Cullercoats.

When first exhibited, however, the assessment of the art press amounted to no more than faint praise. In most respects the painting was a failure, an exceedingly rare one for this artist in midcareer. Homer sought no further showings of the work, and it remained unseen for a decade.

In or around 1892 he extensively rethought and reworked it, apparently motivated by an opportunity to exhibit a new version of the painting in 1893 at the World's Columbian Exposition in Chicago. He reduced much of the canvas leaving only the fishwife and her son, now shown in the midst of a major storm with driving winds. He extensively repainted what remained of the surrounding choppy water, transforming it into a very rough sea. He overpainted the section of the dock on which the fishwife walked, transforming it into a dangerously wet and slippery expanse of rock. He eliminated the coble and the veranda altogether.

From its first showing in Chicago, this radically rethought and repainted version of the painting, which was retitled first as *The Great Gale*, and then in time simply *The Gale*, has met with much critical and popular praise.

The original painting's only surviving parts were the figures of the fishwife and her son. In making alterations to his initial version, Homer trimmed a few inches from the top and the bottom of the canvas to bring these two figures seemingly closer to the viewer. He left the figures themselves largely unchanged, and for this some gratitude is in order, for they constitute a major accomplishment for Homer as a figure painter. The wide-eyed red-headed boy with wind-blown hair remains among the most memorable portrayals of a child in nineteenth-century American painting. Homer's depiction of the fishwife, unconventional as a figure in motion, nonetheless counts as a rare and highly impressive instance of the naturalistic painting of a clothed figure in extreme circumstances, pressing ahead against very strong winds.

Homer's new strengths as a figure painter had of course been observed in 1881 when American critics saw his *Four Fishwives* in New York, but the quite extraordinary pair of exceedingly dissimilar figures in *The Gale* added a more dramatic component to that achievement.

Neither Homer's earlier *Perils* nor his *Watching* had attained (or sought) the sustained dramatic presence that occurs in *The Gale*. *Perils* in its quietness, and *Watching* in its rich elaborations of alarmed behavior, show nothing of a violent storm in action. Homer's *The Gale*, which is much simpler in concept and much more direct in delivering what it has to say, is an image more powerful in emotional content than any other work he had created in Cullercoats. The commanding instinct to save her child makes this fishwife an equal to the storm that howls around her.

8

Beyond the Village

Coursing the Hare, 1881–1882. Oil on canvas. Virginia Museum of Fine Arts, Richmond, Virginia. G&G 1166. (Plate 12)

Bridlington Quay, 1883. Watercolor. Museum of Fine Arts, Boston, Massachusetts. G&G 1164. (Plate 13)

Hark! The Lark, 1882. Oil on canvas, 1882. Milwaukee Art Museum, Milwaukee, Wisconsin. G&G 1101. (Plate 14)

DURING HIS TIME IN ENGLAND, Homer painted at least four works well away from the village of Cullercoats. One of these was his London-based watercolor *The Houses of Parliament*, 1881.[1] The other three, each in its own way, are works based in or relatively close to the North East. All are works of distinctive individuality that show Homer in a new light.

Coursing the Hare stands by itself within the corpus of Homer's Cullercoats work, for it has no obvious connection to any of his other paintings from the village. It does however have a strong connection to hare coursing, a British sporting activity popular during Homer's time in England. Within his Cullercoats work this finely executed painting is at once the most strikingly original in its subject and also the least comprehended in its imagery. Homer's distinctly unconventional approach to his subject encourages this confusion. Nothing is known of the setting or of Homer's motives in painting this work.[2]

While he apparently never sought exhibition of this painting, it seems to have been from its beginning a work of unusual importance to him. Consider for instance his choice to execute this sporting subject in the more expensive and time-consuming medium of oil paint on canvas, rather than as a watercolor on paper. That choice might lead one to suppose that Homer had painted the work to fulfill a commission, but even then one doubts that a devotee of coursing would have encouraged an artist to depict just the moments that Homer recorded. American viewers at museum exhibitions tend to spend relatively little time with *Coursing*, or to pass it by altogether, puzzled by its title and its lack of any apparent pictorial connection to Homer's familiar images.

Hare coursing is a betting sport that remains relatively little known in the United States, a country where the existence of hares has typically ranged by region from relatively few to none. Then too, hares can be confused with rabbits, though the two species differ in both anatomy and behavior. Among other differences, hares are born above ground and spend their lives there, while rabbits reside in burrows. Hares are larger than rabbits and have longer and more powerful hind legs along with much longer ears.[3]

In the United Kingdom, hare coursing is well remembered from its once wide popularity. It is still practiced privately though illegally, for hare coursing in the United Kingdom was banned by law in 2004.

The locale of the painting is unknown. Homer's figures suggest that this coursing event may have occurred on private grounds, perhaps those of a middle-class country house in the North East. Yet the sparseness of pictorial evidence leaves such a reading wholly conjectural.

Explaining Homer's imagery in the painting poses a challenge to any commentator, even those having a close knowledge of hare coursing and its history. This is so owing to Homer's departure in his painting from nearly all conventions that have been used through the ages to depict the sport. Traditional images coming from ancient Egypt, the classical world, and many parts of Europe up to the present have almost without exception presented a lateral view of the pursuit. In these, a running hare is shown in profile some distance ahead of a pair of pursuing sighthounds also shown in profile. Each of the canines will be of a different color or marking.

Homer departs from historical tradition and depicts the chase head-on. He places the just-released hare at the painting's picture plane, turning in panic to begin a side run that may lead to an escape. The hounds who will pursue the hare have just been released. They begin their chase by racing toward the hare (and toward any viewer of Homer's painting as well).

Included along this axis are figures of persons essential to the sport in England, though rarely shown in other depictions of the sport. The two women act as "beaters." Through their actions they seek to deter the hare from escaping its set route. This pathway will lead to a large open field or meadow, exits from which have been blocked. The male figure in the painting's background is the "slipper" who has released the two hounds simultaneously soon after the hare has been set free. His jacket's traditional red color establishes him as the "master of the hunt," a title more familiar in the socially superior and entirely different sport of fox hunting.

In releasing the two sighthounds, the slipper has stepped or been pulled forward and casts his pair of now free leashes (slips) above him to avoid running into them. Homer has them take the form of a graceful midair arabesque.

Controlled spaces such as fields and meadows have traditionally been the setting for depictions of coursing. This is where those who observe the pursuit from the margins wager on which of the two hounds performs better than the other in a standard range of actions. The hound who earns the most points is declared the winner, even if the hare, which is itself an animal of great speed and agility, has outrun both its pursuers and found a way to safety.

Homer's shift of the subject away from the open field and back to the tightly contained space of the start of the event amounted to a radical "take" on the subject. He may have done so because the few seconds at its beginning contained the event's most varied and concentrated pictorial moments.

The painting merits close inspection, for it constitutes a compact triumph of analytic observation by Homer. It would most surely have been seen as such by any patron devoted to the sport.

Two of Homer's four non-Cullercoats English paintings, *Bridlington Quay*, 1883, and *Flamborough Head*, 1882, feature sites in or near Yorkshire's large coastal town of Bridlington. Nearby, the white cliffs of Flamborough Head rise majestically.

In the early 1880s Bridlington's population amounted to some 6,600 persons. The town was larger in every respect than Cullercoats, and it was situated about 110 land miles south of that village. Bridlington thrived as an important center for the shipping of fish and grain. The quantity of Homer's known work from the locale suggests that he might have spent a week or more there.

One purpose of Homer's journey to Bridlington was most likely to take a side-trip to another Yorkshire town, Scarborough, seventeen miles along the coast to the north. His purpose would have been to acquaint himself with the town that had been the source of the name of the village of Scarborough in the state of Maine, the location of his planned Prout's Neck residence and studio. By the early 1880s Prout's was already the site of two Homer family summer homes. In 1884 Homer would move his residence and studio permanently from New York City to his newly constructed Prout's Neck studio/ cottage in Scarborough.

Homer's journey from Cullercoats to Bridlington may have been by sea rather than by rail. Because Maggie Jefferson appears in three of his Bridlington-based works—a fine drawing, an intriguing figure painting, and his *Hark! The Lark*—it seems possible that Homer, Maggie, and perhaps Maggie's mother traveled down the coast as passengers in a sailing vessel with Maggie's father James at the helm. James Jefferson was a well-known Cullercoats mariner. In season he sailed with the Cullercoats fishing fleet. During the off-season he served as a pilot for ships going into or leaving the Port of Tyne, a most exacting responsibility.[4] Though such a voyage down the coast to Bridlington for Homer is conjectural, it remains well within the realm of possibility.

Homer's Bridlington works include a very fine drawing in graphite and watercolor, *Flamborough Head*, 1882 (Art Institute of Chicago). It depicts the massive white chalk cliff that juts into the Atlantic just east of Bridlington. This headland is the largest of its kind in the North of England. Homer would later make use of it in his watercolor *A Voice from the Cliffs* (see chapter 9).

For his watercolor *Bridlington Quay*, Homer posed Maggie Jefferson in her Cullercoats fisherlass attire. She holds a small child in her arms. (Might this child, who had appeared also in *Four Fishwives* and *Beach Scene*, be of Homer's invention, based perhaps on sketches made of a toddler in Homer's Front Street neighborhood?)

An older woman stands in profile next to Maggie. She too is dressed as a fishwife, but in Bridlington colors. Her broadly strapped back carrier is of a kind that makes no appearance in Homer's Cullercoats paintings. As if to emphasize the weights this woman often carried, Homer places on the other side of the two figures a large heavy creel resting to dry on a suspended fishing net. The identity of the older woman is unknown, but speculation suggests among other possibilities that she may be either a Jefferson Bridlington relative or Maggie's mother.

Homer's handling of the two figures is curious. The right-angled positioning of the two women's heads leaves the older woman looking directly at—or even past—Maggie, while Maggie looks forward to the picture plane. This lack of active association between the two figures would have been unusual for Homer in his Cullercoats-sited work. Flesh and hair colors along with a prominent passage of white serve to bring the figures out of the surrounding tans, blues, and grays, with all details showing a rapidity of execution that enlivens this scene of two unmoving women.

The massive forest of ship's masts in the background at left is more dense than any of those Homer had put to use in his Cullercoats Bay paintings. At right a mist-obscured view of the upper levels of some of Bridlington's larger buildings amounts to a rare instance of Homer painting even so much as a detail of an urban scene.

This is a fascinating painting, one held together by Homer's very strong and very moving portrayal of Maggie, not so much as a fisherlass but as a young woman. Indeed, the painting is nothing less than an informal and affectionate portrait of Margaret Jefferson herself. Homer has her step into the open space of the foreground—the painter's space.

Homer's oil painting *Hark! The Lark* was in his view the most important product of his time in England. The painting's inclusion in the 1882 Summer Exhibition of England's Royal Academy of Arts was indeed a distinct honor for an American artist. Established in 1789, the Summer Exhibition was (and remains) unique within London's attention to the fine arts. It was an open submission event in which artist members of the Royal Academy (Academicians) chose the works to be exhibited. Curators, critics, dealers, owners, collectors, and journalists had no say in this selection. For Homer to have had a painting accepted for the exhibition was a major event in his career, one that established him firmly as a "serious" artist. It is curious that the history of his *Hark! The Lark* in America has been very largely as a painting admired and respected, but less loved than its maker's earlier and more distinctly American subjects.[5] *Hark!* is a more somber work than most of his Cullercoats watercolors, with fewer intimations of narrative or community activity.

The Summer Exhibition of 1882 was not the first to include a work by Homer. His 1876 oil painting, *The Cotton Pickers* (Los Angeles County Museum of Art), had been purchased in New York by an English cotton dealer who after returning to England submitted it with success for inclusion in the Royal Academy's Summer Exhibition of 1878.

Homer took *Hark! The Lark*'s title from a song in Shakespeare's *Cymbeline*. That play had enjoyed revivals in England and the United States during the later decades of the nineteenth century. This may have encouraged Homer to presume or hope that critics in America would find in the painting enriching overtones of English literary, theatrical, and musical arts.

The painting is a striking work. It is "heavier" than most of his other Cullercoats paintings, not only in its oil medium but also in the tightness of its composition and the depth of its color. It offers a fascinating comparison to the previous year's *Four Fishwives* in its very different uses of Maggie Jefferson. In the earlier work she is a busy child-minder striding rapidly to work on the sands. In *Hark! The Lark* she becomes three standing young fishwives, presumably sisters, who seem enhanced by the early morning call and flight of a bird. In *Four Fishwives* the figures stride rapidly in full light to the spot on the sands where they are to attend their coble. In *Hark!* Homer has his three figures move momentarily away from their labors, with their thoughts and motions stilled by the bird.

The next year Homer compounded *Hark*'s success by painting an off-shoot of sorts. This was his quite impressive and warmly received watercolor, *A Voice from the Cliffs*. In this he painted a brighter surrounding light, one from later in the morning than that of *Hark*'s darker illumination. He thrice altered Maggie Jefferson's likeness, but only barely, to serve as the painting's three sisters. In both the oil and the watercolor his roughly parallel arrangements of the figures' arms achieve something of the effect of musical variations on a theme.

Though he often left the titling of a painting to an American dealer, in the case of *Hark! The Lark* he chose it himself. He did so in a way that encouraged viewers to move beyond a routinely superficial viewing of the painting's figures to ponder their significance. Homer's three young fisherlasses, already awake and on their way to their labors, elevate their eyes slightly to gain a glimpse of the bird as it flies by. Behind them the day's new light begins to fill the sky.

An element of heaviness in the painting comes from the solid weight of the mound behind the figures and is reinforced by the close grouping of the figures both facially and with their extended arms. He has also given each figure an individual sense of alertness that distinguishes her from the others.

On more than one occasion late in his career Homer referred to *Hark! The Lark* as "the most important picture I ever painted, and the very best one, as the figures are large enough to have some expression in their faces."[6] He made similar claims of importance now and then for a few other works, but *Hark!* was by many measures a work superior to them. As an artist who had little concern with the verbal analysis of works of art, Homer's brief and simple observation about the scale of the figures and their facial expressions makes one wonder in what ways he might have described the painting in its entirety.

In categorizing this work as "important" he may have had in mind the existence of a higher, more stable, and purer standard of critical judgment than that of the art press or the implications of dollars earned from a sale. He may have been thinking only of something as simple as an honor conferred. For *Hark! The Lark* to have been selected for exhibition by the Royal Academy, an institution whose history and stature far surpassed that of any American art organization, was indeed an honor.

9

Culmination

A Voice from the Cliffs, 1883. Watercolor. Private Collection. G&G 1170. (Plate 15)

The Incoming Tide, 1883. Watercolor. American Academy of Arts and Letters, New York City, New York. G&G 1173. (Plate 16)

Inside the Bar, 1883. Watercolor. Metropolitan Museum of Art, New York City, New York. G&G 1172. (Plate 17)

Returning Fishing Boats (originally titled *Tynemouth*), 1883. Watercolor. Harvard Art Museums, Fogg Museum, Cambridge, Massachusetts. G&G 1169. (Plate 18)

An Afterglow, 1883. Watercolor. Museum of Fine Arts, Boston, Massachusetts. G&G 1180. (Plate 19)

WHEN HOMER returned to New York in late November 1882, he was keenly aware that the large body of paintings and drawings that he had produced in Cullercoats remained almost entirely unknown to his fellow Americans. The American press had taken scant interest in his activities during his time abroad. Even so, Homer surely harbored hopes that his work from England would be warmly received. He can have had few doubts concerning the potential value of these paintings and drawings in the market for works in fine arts. His confidence in the quality of his work never flagged.

In New York he settled again in Washington Square close to his parents, his older brother Charles, and Charles's wife Mattie. He once more shared an apartment in the Benedick Building with Samuel Thorndyke Preston ("Thorny" to family and friends). Preston was Mattie's cousin. Over the years he had been a virtual cousin as well to the three Homer brothers. Homer had used Preston's New York business address (he was a dealer in animal skins) when shipping paintings and drawings from England to New York.

For studio space, Homer arranged a return to the Tenth Street Studio Building. He knew that facility well, having worked there throughout most of the 1870s. He would make use of his studio in the building during the summer and autumn of 1883 when he painted the first of his post-Cullercoats oils, *The Life Line* (Plate 20).

In December 1882 and early January 1883, Homer applied finishing touches to the four Cullercoats watercolors he had painted for inclusion in the American Watercolor Society's sixteenth annual exhibition of members' new work, which opened to critics and the public in January 1883. In the same weeks he brought to completion a few other watercolors he began working on in Cullercoats, dating them all "1883" though he may have started them as much as a year earlier.

In the course of his final months in the village, Homer must have closely considered the nature of the works he would place in the New York exhibition. He had miscalculated on that score the previous year when in January 1882 critics had so actively disliked his *Four Fishwives*.

Consequently, in preparing the four watercolors that would represent him in the 1883 exhibition, Homer largely avoided depictions of fishwives' labors but maintained fishwives themselves as his paintings' key figures. He gave the sea a new sense of prominence in all four works, doing so differently in each case. The four watercolors he selected for exhibition were *A Voice from the Cliffs*, *The Incoming Tide*, *Inside the Bar*, and *Returning Fishing Boats*. Each of the four differed from its companions in subject, mood, composition, and dramatic effect.

Because the response of critics to this quartet was extraordinarily positive (as discussed in chapter 2), Homer undoubtedly found himself in January 1883 to be a more fully and deeply respected artist than at any time since the Civil War. The praise that critics showered on the four watercolors must have gone far to make up for the occasional slights, grumbles, reservations, and outright complaints that had appeared now and then in art press reviews of his paintings.

Perceptive American viewers would have been struck by the "newness" of his Cullercoats work. His enlightened images of working women, for instance, were bold for their time in depicting what amounted to the "new woman" of the English working class. Another watercolor that Homer had very likely begun in Cullercoats but dated 1883 was *An Afterglow*. Because this work contains strengths on a par with those of the four he sent to the Watercolor Society's exhibition, it can be considered with them, displaying Homer's virtuosity as he concluded his time in England. The five also serve as a gesture of affection for a place, a people, and a way of life that Homer would never see again.

A Voice from the Cliffs, with its enigmatic title, was Homer's adaptation of major elements from his 1882 oil painting *Hark! The Lark* (see chapter 8). It is perhaps a sign of his great confidence in what he had created in that earlier work that he produced such an effective semblance of its key components using a new medium and color scheme. He altered major and minor details while preserving the essential form and mood of its group of three figures. His use of watercolor created a new freshness and intimacy overall, while it also preserved a sense of the oil's seriousness of mood. Entirely new was his addition of a view of the sea at both right and left, each containing a single sail-rigged boat. This pair of marine details added pictorial interest while it also brought the sea into close view.

In his painting *Hark! The Lark,* Homer had set the figures before an expanse of the early light of dawn. In *A Voice* this depiction becomes instead a massive wall of white chalk glowing in the morning's brightening light, as at Flamborough Head. His new title shifted the apparent time from the fresh dawn of *Hark!* to the somewhat fuller light of early morning. In *A Voice,* the light envelops the setting to give it a sense of fresh new life. While the source of the title's "voice" is left undefined, it could be taken as that of a fellow worker calling to these figures. More likely, perhaps, it is a device to invest the new light itself with a summoning strength.

In composing the new image, Homer removed a creel that in the oil had protruded between the shoulders of the two fisherlasses at right. In doing this he strengthened the individuality of each figure and reinforced the watercolor's horizontal orientation. The oil's vertical emphasis had been in concert with the upturned eyes of its figures surprised by the overhead flight of the lark. By trimming the original image's proportions at top and bottom, Homer gave the watercolor a stronger left-to-right emphasis that brought the three figures seemingly closer to the viewer.

Lost with these changes was *Hark! The Lark*'s impressive formality. Lost as well was the earlier painting's touch of drama in its figures' faces. But these are minor differences.

The Watercolor Society commissioned Homer to make a small-scale line drawing of *A Voice from the Cliffs* for reproduction on the cover of the 1883 exhibition catalogue. In making the drawing Homer reduced and further simplified the basic image while he preserved essential strengths from the original painting. His three-stage success in presenting these fisherlasses in oil, watercolor, and line had few if any precedents in the work of other American artists of his time. In sum, Homer did not revise his *Hark! The Lark* when he painted *A Voice from the Cliffs* so much as he reinvented it. *A Voice* remains a major work of nineteenth-century American painting in watercolors in both concept and execution.

In Homer's *The Incoming Tide*, a fishwife walks steadily, intently, and with determined assurance up the wet sands directly toward the viewer. She stays scarcely a few steps ahead of the slowly rising seawater. The weight of the heavy load lodged on her right shoulder has caused her to shift her upper body slightly to the left to counterbalance it. She looks to the left not only because her head is now partly oriented in that direction but also to note the bit of debris the tide has just delivered. Homer sets the regular rhythm of her steps against the irregular surges of the waves behind her. She is a solid upright in a horizontal setting of movement. The panorama of cloud and breaking waves is among Homer's most effective.

Dramatically imperturbable, this fishwife's straight-ahead boldness speaks of self-confidence and independence. In the distance a coble with a raised sail adds a second vertical element to the composition, but without in any way diminishing the primacy of the fishwife.

Homer here enlarges on what he had introduced a year earlier with the figures in his *Four Fishwives*. In that painting he had captured laterally a moment in the four figures' forward movement. In *The Incoming Tide* he presents frontally the movement of a single figure, an even more challenging task owing to the foreshortenings required. The figure heads directly toward its viewer, perhaps arousing a fleeting inclination among some to step aside and let her pass. His *Four Fishwives* had been about group behavior and working together as a team, but *The Incoming Tide* moves beyond that to show the strengths of the individual. The background's moving water and wind-driven clouds contribute a sense of irregular motion, which through contrast reinforces the fishwife's fixed pace. The angled diagonal of the oncoming water's edge may arouse concern that the tide will soon catch up with her boots, but Homer assures the viewer through his quite confident and fine-tuned draughtsmanship that *his* tide will not reach *his* fishwife.

Homer was especially pleased with this figure. She appears in several of his drawings in which he varies background details while changing little of the figure itself. Her confident determination survives in each variant. This watercolor is in several respects the simplest of the paintings Homer placed in the 1883 exhibition and perhaps also the most memorable.

The imposing figure who dominates the work *Inside the Bar* proved to be for critics of the time the strongest image in the exhibition. Little more than a century later, in 1988, the image regained much of that distinction when it appeared on the cover of the catalogue of the illuminating exhibition *Winslow Homer: All the Cullercoats Pictures* mounted at the Centre of Contemporary Art in Sunderland, County Durham, a few miles along the coast south of Cullercoats.

At least a few persons in the North East may have for the first time seen paintings in this exhibition or in its catalogue for which a grandparent or great-grandparent posed. On October 9, 1988, the Sunderland exhibition received a strongly positive review in the Manchester Guardian Weekly from the newspaper's distinguished art critic, Tim Hilton. He cites Homer's frankness, humanity, lack of pretension, and disregard of precedent. Hilton also praised Homer's watercolor technique, calling it superior to that of most English users of the medium.[1] Homer had developed *Inside the Bar* from his exhibition drawing of 1881, *Windy Day, Cullercoats*, graphite and gouache on tan paper (Portland Museum of Art). From that drawing he took not only the painting's basic concept, composition, and organization of detail but also the imposing figure of its fishwife with her wind-blown attire. The boldness of Homer's uses of blue and white was something rather new, a move that gave his watercolor strength. Here and there he added small-scale appearances of contrasting local color, such as the red of the fishwife's scarf that calls attention to her face.

The painting attracted much praise at the Watercolor Society's exhibition. Several months later its cover image became a further hallmark of that event when Marianna Van Rensselaer used a small outline drawing of the painting along with a tonal photograph of its central figure to illustrate the work in her article about Homer in *The Century*.

Discussions of the painting have often noted how the curving shape of the figure's apron echoes the coble's wind-blown sail (or vice versa), and how each seems to be descended from the bowed handle of this fishwife's creel. Homer may have meant her confident stance to signify her community's multiple strengths, but even so it is interesting that he should choose a single commanding figure to represent such a distinctly community-oriented population.

His figure stands confidently on what seems to be a reef of rock near Cullercoats Bay's sandbar. The sea is alive with movement, a suggestion perhaps of the figure's barely contained energy. She is an imagined rather than idealized figure, memorable for her naturalistically elevated left foot. Her image has sometimes served to support arguments that Homer in England,

and most likely while at the British Museum, became so impressed by works of classical sculpture that he idealized certain of his fishwives accordingly. This supposition weakens however as one seeks in his Cullercoats figures evidence of the classical style's expectations of a harmony and simplicity of parts, balanced proportions, restraint of expression, and other essential qualities.

Homer's figure may seem to be almost a study for a monument, but he has invested her with much that is nonmonumental, not least her wind-driven apron and her tilted foot. The degree of flamboyance in her figure seems more a product of the stage than the studio. She proves nonetheless to be an agreeable companion to those nearby.

The figure's theatricality is a late development in Homer's Cullercoats manner. It stands in sharp contrast to, say, the well-defined naturalism of his younger fishwife with child in arms in his earlier *Watching from the Cliffs* (Plate 2). That painting's intimacy of mother and child would have no counterpart in the grandly public mood of *Inside the Bar*.

Homer's treatment of that later painting's light in its varying intensities, especially as reflected from the surface of the bay's water, unifies the composition. As a balance to the prominent central figure, he has added to the scene a coble that sails ahead. Even the dory closer to this grand-scale fishwife shows signs of movement. The upright figures in the coble present an effective contrast to those sitting or slouching in the dory. Might Homer here suggest that the coble's occupants have been called to action with their community fellows, while those in the dory have not yet heard this fishwife's summons?

Behind all this the wind builds up a bank of moving grey cloud rising to serve as a silhouetting arched backdrop for the main figure. The texture Homer gives the wind-blown cloud and its surround of dark sky is in vivid contrast to the flat rock surfaces that support the most monumental of his fishwives.

The 1883 exhibition featured a watercolor by Homer that bore the title *Tynemouth*. It later came to be known as *Sailing Home at Sunset, Tynemouth* until it at last acquired its present title, *Returning Fishing Boats*. The prominence in the painting of the smoke-emitting trawler confirms Tynemouth as the subject's site, for that town's docks served the trawlers of this part of the North Sea coast. In a few earlier works, including *Breakwater, Cullercoats*, Homer had placed the profile of a trawler on the distant horizon, but he had only rarely given such bold prominence to one of these controversial ships.

The painting's earlier title, *Sailing Home at Sunset*, made its subject clear. This coble with its occupants, as well as those in the coble some distance ahead, are sailing back to Cullercoats, three miles north along the coast. The last of light from the setting sun may suffice to get them to the bay before dusk.

The coble's empty creels suggest that its two fishermen have made a delivery to Tynemouth where the two young fishwives would have taken the contents of the boat's creels to waiting dealers at the fish market. Here, more than in any of his earlier Cullercoats work, Homer depicts fishwives and fishermen working together, as of course they always had. This is a painting not so much about community as about friendly cooperation. A great wind-filled sail pulls them home.

Of Homer's four paintings in the 1883 exhibition, *Returning Fishing Boats* in many respects came closest to the spirit and appearances of the fisherfolk community that Homer knew and selectively painted. The two young fishwives hold on together for balance as their coble moves along in choppy water. Homer presents the fishermen in more detail than usual, perhaps to at last bring them together with the women pictorially.

The choppy water of the painting's foreground with its quickly done waves sporting light blue peaks suits the subject. How interesting that this placid, almost decorative detail should be one of Homer's last painted passages of moving seawater before he left Cullercoats. He would follow it up in New York a few months later with the ferociously active high sea of his oil painting *The Life Line* (Plate 21). If one must seek a turning point at this stage of Homer's development, it is surely to be found in that New York–based product of his 1883 spring/summer visits to the New Jersey coast and its life-saving practices.

An Afterglow offers a warm sense of the quiet pleasures that might accompany relaxed moments spent among fellow fisherfolk. It also concerns the visual rewards that might come from the labors of a life spent among cobles. Here breezes lift the sail of the coble at left to frame the boat's two fishwives. A single figure in the other boat offers a likeness of Maggie Jefferson. This may be Homer's concluding attention to his able associate.

The painting is also a display of Homer's great strengths as a painter in transparent watercolors. These strengths appear prominently in his treatment of the reflected light of the gently moving waters in the painting's foreground. The whiteness of the watercolor paper works together with Homer's pigments on the brushed, scraped, and otherwise manipulated surface textures of the work. He extends this painterly treatment into the background, steadily adjusting it for scale, distance, and intensity of color as he carries it to the horizon.

The hues of the foreground water also serve the massive sky of the background, but with different results. This sky rises from the horizon with borrowings of colors from the water to become a dark and tumultuously threatening sky. The contrast between the quietly engaged young fishwives chatting near still waters and the mammoth clouds that threaten in the distance transform what seems at first glance to be a conventional scene.

Two cobles at center sail into the middle ground. They tie the composition together by occupying a space that is an extension of the one that separates the two foreground cobles. At far left a group of cobles sails toward the horizon. Homer presents the group not as part of the village's fishing fleet so much as cobles in more casual use.

That all the painting's vessels appear to be sailing away may reflect its maker's understanding that he too would soon be leaving. He would not depart by coble but by the NER to connections that would deliver him and his baggage to Liverpool and a steamship for New York.

The green-coated man who bends forward in the coble may be a father, husband, or other relative of one or more of the young fishwives. Homer drew this figure more carefully and thoughtfully than he did most of his Cullercoats males. He makes the figure's coat into a small essay in paint on how differing values and intensities of the color green can add visual interest to such ordinary objects. The coat also serves as a component of the painting's compositional structure. Its body of green serves to anchor and balance a lighter green-yellow corner of sky above at upper right.

The mood of relaxed pleasure among friends that pervades this painting is one unseen in Homer's earlier Cullercoats paintings and rare even in his later American work. It may well reflect its maker's outlook and thinking as he prepared to leave Cullercoats.

IO

Aftermath

The Life Line, 1884. Oil on canvas. Philadelphia Museum of Art, Philadelphia, Pennsylvania. G&G 1218. (Plate 20)

THE GREAT SUCCESS of Homer's 1883 Cullercoats watercolors lost much of its luster within a year, upstaged by none other than Homer himself. Once back in the United States, he found a new subject of major interest with little connection to anything he had painted while in the village. His new subject's roots ran not to Cullercoats but to Atlantic City, New Jersey. There, in the spring or summer of 1883, he witnessed demonstrations of new breeches buoy life-saving equipment. A trained crew of coastguardsmen demonstrated the uses of the apparatus. From this experience, and bolstered by his imagination and powers of invention, Homer developed his oil painting *The Life Line*. This was a dramatic work unlike any he had created in England or elsewhere, and it became a stunning success when exhibited at the National Academy in New York in March 1884.

He had worked on *The Life Line* in studio space at the Tenth Street Studio Building, using professional models for the painting's two figures. In the painting he suspends both figures over a very rough sea. Critics gave the painting a glowingly positive reception, though a few of them surely harbored reservations about Homer's positioning of his figures. Even before that, a well-respected collector had bought the painting for the handsome sum of $2,500. This was by far the largest amount paid for any Homer painting up to that time.

Homer's initial thinking about his new subject may have been sparked by memory of an event near Cullercoats that he had observed, sketched, and developed into his watercolor, *The Wreck of the Iron Crown*, 1881 (Baltimore Museum of Art). The *Iron Crown* was a ship that had run aground in October 1881 while seeking entry to the Port of Tyne. The news of the wreck had spread quickly to Cullercoats and drew Homer to coastal heights overlooking the ship. He arrived just as the Tynemouth Lifesaving Brigade in its lifeboat approached the wreck to save the last person still remaining on board. This they did by means of a breeches buoy.

In depicting the Lifesaving Brigade's approach to the ship, Homer revived some of his reportorial instincts from the late 1850s and 1870s that had spelled his success as a freelance artist for the pictorial press. Yet the two paintings differ so extensively that it makes little sense to think of the earlier work as a significant source for *The Life Line*. The differences are marked: one depicts the accurate documentation of an event and the other suggests an imagined moment meant to capture its viewer's attention. The differences leave the *Iron Crown* as a highly interesting documentary work of Homer's midcareer, but not one that contributed substantially to his strikingly original *Life Line*.

That painting depicts a pair of entwined figures suspended above a rough sea. One is an unconscious, fully dressed woman. The other is a manly coastguardsman whose face Homer has covered by the woman's wind-blown scarf. The coastguardsman sits in a breeches buoy suspended from its hawser, holding the woman closely and safely as the two are pulled to shore.

Homer's angle of vision in this painting is that of a person levitating in midair close to the two suspended figures. Some of his earlier seas had been quite rough, with such large troughs and sharply peaked waves as appear in his *Life Line*.

The successes of 1883 and 1884 made Homer an American painter of steadily growing importance. They also gave him the means and confidence to abandon New York and its art communities and to settle permanently in his newly completed cottage/studio at Prout's Neck. From "Prouts" he with some regularity brought or sent to his dealers fresh works of importance on new subjects. He had painted these not only in the United States but also in Quebec and the Bahamas. Only very rarely, as in his oil painting *Cloud Shadows* of 1890 (Spencer Museum of Art, University of Kansas), do faint echoes of Homer in England's North East survive. A few figural subjects from Maine, such as that of his oil painting *Fisher Girl*, 1894 (Mead Museum of Art, Amherst College), depict a subject that can be categorized as an American equivalent of a Cullercoats fishwife. But *Fisher Girl* possesses none of the energy, individuality, or involvement with others that enlivens the fishwives Homer painted in England.

For two years following *The Life Line*, Homer took as his primary subject North Atlantic fishermen and other mariners, often situated on large ships and sometimes in troublesome weather or worse. The mood in oil paintings such as his quite fine *Eight Bells*, 1886 (Addison Gallery of American Art, Phillips Academy) seems impersonal compared to the moods of his Cullercoats watercolors, though *Eight Bells* reaches greater depths of seriousness in its subject and of confidence in its execution as a painting.

In 1887 Homer's oil painting *Undertow* (Sterling and Francine Clark Art Institute) repeated the critical, popular, and financial success of *The Life Line*. In his newer painting, two hardy coastguardsmen, one bare-breasted, rescue two semiconscious young women in bathing attire who have been overcome while in heavy breaking waves. There was much good painting in all these works, but also enough melodramatic narrative to distract from Homer's achievements on canvas. None contained the close and casual association of persons so typical of his Cullercoats paintings.

In 1889, well settled at Prout's Neck, Homer returned to the Adirondacks after an absence of a dozen years. He began by spending early May to mid-July of that year at the North Woods Club (formerly the Baker Farm), and then returned to Prout's Neck for most of the months of October and November. This began a new and richly productive period in a region where between 1870 and 1877 he had painted a strong and well-received body of Adirondack-sited oils and watercolors. In those he had captured much of the look and life of the region's lakes, forests, mountains, and "locals." His oil painting *The Two Guides* of 1877 (Sterling and Francine Clark Art Institute) remains a major work of his earlier time "in the woods."

After Cullercoats, Homer's Adirondack subjects became more varied and his paintings larger and more richly accomplished in the uses of transparent watercolor.[1] Among them were such masterful works as *An October Day*, 1889 (Sterling and Francine Clark Art Institute); *Mink Pond*, 1891 (Harvard Art Museums, Fogg Museum); and *The Adirondack Guide*, 1894 (Museum of Fine Arts, Boston). These are most impressive paintings, but in new ways. They show little if anything reminiscent of his time in Cullercoats or anywhere else. He had always been an artist who worked episodically, becoming in each significant episode a "new artist."

After Cullercoats, women infrequently appear in Homer's paintings, but when they do they tend to be memorable. They differed pictorially not only from his fishwives but also among themselves from painting to painting. In his *A Summer Night*, 1890 (Musée d'Orsay, Paris), two women dance on the porch of a Prout's Neck summer house while other figures sit nearby watching a display of moonlight on the sea. This is in every respect a more complex work than any Homer had painted while in England.

Homer's winter visits to Florida and the Caribbean in the 1880s and 1890s occasionally brought forth effective figures of women in native dress quietly engaged with their surroundings. This ended his painting of women at least as subjects for exhibition. One wonders to what extent, if at all, Homer thought back to, or in any way recalled, his time in Cullercoats. He had always been a person very largely concerned with the present rather than the past.

Homer died at Prout's Neck in 1910 a few weeks following his last stay in the Adirondacks. Three years later, in 1913, the Armory Show in New York City introduced major aspects of European Modernism to American audiences. The impact of the exhibition spelled an end to much that had been deemed important in nineteenth-century American painting, but Homer's half century of work, including his many Cullercoats paintings, proved to be among the major exceptions to this great and profound shift in American taste.

Notes

Bibliography

Index

Notes

Acknowledgments

1. Harrison, Tony. *Winslow Homer in England*. Ocean Park, Maine: Hornby Editions, 1983.

1. Introduction

1. In Paris he studied with no master. Through independent visits to the Louvre and contemporary galleries he absorbed aspects of the manner and mood of French naturalistic painting of his time. He did so without acquiring significant lasting aspects of any particular French manner.

2. David Tatham, *Winslow Homer in London* (Syracuse: Syracuse Univ. Press, 2010), 29–40.

3. William Howe Downes, *The Life and Work of Winslow Homer* (Boston: Houghton Mifflin, 1911), 106. Lloyd Goodrich, *Winslow Homer* (New York: Macmillan, 1944), 82.

4. Peasantry in England had very largely died out by the early decades of the sixteenth century. Elizabeth I freed the last remaining serfs in 1574. Nor were the Cullercoats fisher-folk, who had settled by invitation at the bay in the 1740s, "peasant-like," that is, uneducated, ignorant, or unfamiliar with the urban world. They were, both male and female, literate and highly skilled workers. Many of the men owned or leased their boats and in good seasons experienced comfortable earnings. Cullercoats Bay was essentially their exclusive preserve, as were their fishing grounds in the North Sea. Most of the Cullercoats fisherfolk were members of the village's Primitive Methodist Church, a sect strongly opposed to all aspects of the peasantry system. In view of the fisherfolk's sense of organization and efficiency, it makes sense to view them as part of an offshoot of the Industrial Revolution as it had developed in the North East rather than as a survival of folk culture.

2. Homer as a "New Artist"

1. The four paintings were *A Voice from the Cliffs* (Plate 15); *Inside the Bar* (Plate 17); *The Incoming Tide* (Plate 16); and *Tynemouth*, now known as *Returning Fishing Boats* (Plate 18), all dated 1883. These paintings are discussed in chapter 9.

2. Lloyd Goodrich and Abigail Booth Gerdts, *Record of Works by Winslow Homer*, vol. 4.1 (New York: Homer Art Education Project, 2005–2014).

3. Marianna Griswold Van Rensselaer, "The Watercolor Exhibition, New York," *American Architect and Building News* 12 (March 24, 1883): 138.

4. Marianna Griswold Van Rensselaer, "An American Artist in England," *The Century*, November 1883, 13–21.

5. Lucretia Hoover Giese, "Winslow Homer's 'Better Painting': *Old Woman Gathering Faggots*, 1865," *Visual Resources* 27, no. 1 (2011): 63–76.

3. England's North East

1. For a survey of his locations and activities, see David Tatham, *Winslow Homer in London* (Syracuse: Syracuse Univ. Press, 2010).

2. The Earls of Northumberland had existed between 1377 and 1749, with succession in each generation belonging to the eldest male of the Percy family line. Perhaps the most widely known account of a member of this family is that by Shakespeare of Sir Henry Percy (1364–1403), heir to the Earldom and the model for Hotspur in *Henry IV, Part 1*. Homer may have known the play, for it was performed often in New York during the post–Civil War decades owing in good part to its richly comic character of Falstaff. In 1766, some years after the extinction of the Earldom owing to a lack of a Percy male heir, the noble hereditary title of Duke of Northumberland came into being. Here too the Dukes in each generation have been the eldest son in the Percy line, one that continues to the present.

3. The North East had become an official Region of England in 1972, though the phrase "North East" had been in common use for generations earlier. The region's boundaries included the historic counties of Northumberland and Durham and part of North Yorkshire.

4. The present author's knowledge of the tradition comes from an informal discussion luncheon hosted by the Essex Institute in Salem, Massachusetts in the early 1970s in which the topic was American artists working abroad. When one participant asked, "Why did Winslow Homer go to England?" a voice (unrecognized by the present writer) responded without pause to the effect that Homer had a commission from someone in New York.

5. Since 1950 this church has been a Grade I Listed Building in the National Heritage list for England, ensuring its preservation.

6. David Tatham, "*General Giuseppe Garibaldi*, an Unrecorded *Harper's Weekly* Illustration by Winslow Homer," *Imprint* 26, no. 2 (Autumn 2001): 32–33. See also David Tatham, *Winslow Homer and the Pictorial Press* (Syracuse: Syracuse Univ. Press, 2003), 94–99.

4. Homer's Cullercoats

1. Tradition holds that Homer throughout his stay occasionally dined at the village's hotel or enjoyed a drink in its lounge.

2. Founded in 1824, the National Lifeboat Institute had in 1866 received a Royal Charter in recognition of its many years of work in saving lives at sea. It had established Lifeboat Stations around the coasts of the United Kingdom, all manned by volunteers. The institute remains one of that nation's most respected charities. During Homer's time in the village the stations at both Cullercoats and Tynemouth, which were among the earliest established nationally, saw much activity from the traffic of ships and boats in and out of the Port of Tyne.

3. These two cottages along with the other fisherfolk cottages on Front Street probably dated from the 1840s. The ground floor of 44B apparently consisted of a single room with

a stone floor and range for heat and cooking. A shared washroom stood outside the building on a back lane.

4. The men locate this boat well up on the sands in advance of an oncoming storm and an unusually high tide. The fishermen have undoubtedly helped to beach other cobles and will soon move on to more. The fisherman to the left, who has done his part elsewhere on the sands, runs with his sack of boat gear toward a wide ramped roadway (beyond the drawing's margin) leading to Front Street and his family. Homer's vigorous figure drawing and broken areas of reflected light on wet sand reinforce the mood of the moment.

5. William Weaver Tomlinson, *The North Eastern Railway: Its Rise and Development* (Devon: Newton Abbott, 1915).

6. William Weaver Tomlinson, *Historical Notes on Cullercoats, Whitley and Monkseaton, with a Descriptive Memoir of the Coast from Tynemouth to St. Mary's Island* (London: Walter Scott, 1893), 110–11.

7. The present-day local historian, Lloyd Reed (no relation to Cleota Reed), seems to be the first to have reported a belief that Carrick's father, the artist Thomas Heathfield Carrick (1802–1874), had built and maintained a ground-level studio near No. 12 Banktop. Lloyd G. Reed, *Cullercoats Village 1292–1950* (Raleigh, NC: Lulu Editions, 2014), 5.

8. Because the street wall prevented direct access to the described studio building from Bank Top, or even the sight of a studio, Homer or any visitor to the facility would have needed first to enter No. 12 Bank Top, pass through its ground level into No. 13, and from there exit into the outdoor space containing the studio. If Homer used the Carrick studio regularly, his repeated entries into and exits from No. 12 on his way to and from the studio would very likely have left an impression on passersby that he had routine business in that building. If Homer had rented the Carrick studio he may also have rented the second-level room in No. 12 Bank Top not as a studio but as storage space for art supplies and paintings in progress.

9. William Adamson, *Newcastle-upon-Tyne* (Newcastle upon Tyne: Robert Robinson, 1877).

10. I thank Kay Easson, Librarian of the Newcastle Literary and Philosophical Society, for providing information about William Adamson as a member of the society.

11. Collection, Royal National Lifeboat Institution Archives.

12. Tony Harrison, "Homer's Friendship with Alan Adamson," in *Winslow Homer in England*, edited by Tony Harrison (Ocean Park, ME: Hornby Editions, 2004), 31–32. The letter is reproduced on p. 32. Harrison does not say where he obtained it, but it is probably from the Adamson family.

13. Alan Adamson, "The Homer That I Knew," in *Winslow Homer in England*, edited by Tony Harrison (Ocean Park, ME: Hornby Editions, 2004), 33–38. Alan Adamson's long life stands in contrast to those of all but one of his siblings. His older brother Bryan, an officer in the Royal Navy, had on September 10, 1887 sailed from Singapore on the *HMS Wasp* as its lieutenant and commander. The ship was a year-old Dreadnaught (battle cruiser) heading for Shanghai and Hong Kong. It was never seen again. The *HMS Wasp* most likely had encountered the typhoon reported on September 19 to have been moving through the western Pacific. The ship and its crew of seventy-five officers and men were lost at sea.

Friends of the Adamsons commissioned a memorial drinking fountain (1888) overlooking Cullercoats Bay and the sea on the broad pavement directly across from the family's

Garden House. The Duke of Northumberland donated the site. Rising on an octagonal plinth of sandstone and marble with cast iron details, its prominently capped white spire seen against blues of the sea or sky easily captures the attention of passersby. The monument survives, showing only modest wear from the years. In 1891, Constance Adamson died at age forty. Her mother Hannah and her father William died in the same year. Their daughter Elinor may have predeceased all the others. The youngest child, Augusta Ann Adamson Mitchell born in 1864, lived a long life, passing away in 1951 at age eighty-six. Nothing is known to suggest that after leaving the village Homer remained in touch with any of the Adamsons.

14. For the art colony see Laura Newton, with Abigail Booth Gerdts, *Cullercoats, a North East Colony of Artists* (Bristol: Sansom & Co., 2003). See also Laura Newton, editor and contributor, *Painting at the Edge: British Coastal Art Colonies 1880–1930* (Bristol: Sansom & Co., 2005). A. B. Gerdts in a chapter in the earlier of these volumes discusses Winslow Homer in America but does not illustrate his Cullercoats paintings. Newton's highly insightful chapters in both books constitute a comprehensive summary of the regional art world Homer would have known in England's North East. Newton's selection of illustrations is invaluable for what it shows of late-nineteenth-century British provincial painting.

5. Fishwives

1. William R. Cross, Exhibition Catalogue, *Homer at the Beach: A Marine Painter's Journey 1869–1880* (Gloucester, MA: Cape Ann Museum, 2019).

2. For instance, in his watercolor *Fisherfolk in a Dory*, 1881 (Harvard University Museums, Fogg Art Museum), he depicts a young fishwife sitting in a dory's stern looking back to land or to another boat while three fishermen, each with a bowed head that obscures his features, attend to matters within the boat.

3. Longstanding fishwife traditions are succinctly summarized in this undated, well-illustrated essay, "The Life of the Cullercoats Fishwife," website essay, Sunniside Local History Society, Sunniside near Newcastle upon Tyne, UK, n.d., www.sunnisidelocalhistorysociety .co.uk.

4. Such anxieties had in the early 1870s become a much-visited subject for Cullercoats painters and others. Among the most admired in its time was H. H. Emmerson's *Waiting for the Boats*, 1870, oil on canvas, private collection. It presents two women, one aged and one young—clearly enough an overdue fisherman's mother and wife—who wait for his coble. For a discussion of the popularity of this subject among English painters see Laura Newton, *Cullercoats, A North East Colony of Artists* (Bristol: Sanson & Co., 2003), 116–17.

5. An oil Homer had painted a year earlier in Gloucester, Massachusetts, *Dad's Coming!* (National Gallery of Art), has a somewhat similar subject, but it differs so extensively in its details and emotional character that it cannot be claimed as a model for the Cullercoats painting.

6. Lloyd G. Reed, *Cullercoats Village 1292–1950* (Raleigh, NC: Lulu Editions, 2014), 246.

7. The 1871 National Census lists James Jefferson and his wife Isabella's seven children and their ages thusly: John, 28; Catherine, 19; Thomas, 16; Barbara, 14; Elizabeth, 11; Isabella, 9; and Margaret, 2. Reed, *Cullercoats Village*, 6. The gap in the otherwise regular birth intervals between Catherine and Margaret is best explained by a misreading in Margaret's case of the census-taker's 7 as a 2. This would make her age 16 or 17 when Homer met her.

8. See Tony Harrison, *Winslow Homer in England* (Ocean Park, ME: Hornby Editions, 2004), 6 and fig. 12.

9. Reed, *Cullercoats Village*, 61, 62.

10. Reed, *Cullercoats Village*, 62.

6. On and above the Sands

1. Lloyd Goodrich, *Winslow Homer* (New York: Macmillan, 1944), 77.

2. David Tatham, *Winslow Homer and the Pictorial Press* (Syracuse: Syracuse Univ. Press, 2003), 57, 58. 61.

3. See for instance Turner's *Tynemouth Priory Seen from the South*, 1797–1798, pencil and watercolor, Tate Gallery, Turner Bequest.

7. Storm

1. See for instance Hugh Graham, "Storm Watching," *Times of London*, Travel Section, October 26, 2010, 3.

2. *Passing a Wreck—Mid Ocean*, 1884, oil on canvas, Colby College Museum of Art, Lunder Collection, G&G 1288.

3. *Perils of the Sea* or *Eternal Father, Strong to Save*, with text by William Whiting (1860) and music by J. R. Dykes (1861), gained widespread popularity first in England and soon afterward in the United States and elsewhere. It became the naval hymn for several nations, and was also often part of Sunday services on ocean liners.

4. The New York printers of Homer's etchings were first George W. H. Ritchie and later Charles S. White. For the etchings, see Lloyd Goodrich, *The Graphic Art of Winslow Homer* (New York: Museum of Graphic Art, 1968), 13–17.

5. The paintings are in the Bowdoin College Art Collections. The image is reproduced in Elizabeth Athens's chapter, "The Gale," in Elizabeth Athens, Brandon Rudd, and Martha Tedeschi, *Coming Away: Winslow Homer in England* (New Haven: Yale Univ. Press, 2017), 36.

8. Beyond the Village

1. Hirshhorn Museum and Sculpture Garden, Smithsonian Institution. For commentary on Homer's *The Houses of Parliament*, see David Tatham, *Homer in London* (Syracuse: Syracuse Univ. Press, 2010), 67–77, pl. 10.

2. For a substantial and informed discussion of the painting see Malcolm Cormack, *Country Pursuits* (Richmond: Virginia Museum of Fine Arts, 2007).

3. In the later decades of the nineteenth century, American sportsmen sometimes substituted jackrabbits for hares. See "Coursing in America," *The Illustrated American*, April 1896, 430–31. I thank Randall Bond for directing me to this source, and also to Frederic Remington's fictional "Coursing Rabbits on the Plains," *Outlook*, May 1887, 111–21.

4. Lloyd G. Reed, *Cullercoats Village 1292–1950* (Raleigh, NC: Lulu Editions, 2014), 246.

5. For commentaries on both *The Gale* and *Hark! The Lark*, see Elizabeth Athens and Brandon Rudd with Martha Tedeschi, *Coming Away: Winslow Homer in England* (New Haven: Yale Univ. Press, 2017).

6. Lloyd Goodrich, *Winslow Homer* (New York: Macmillan, 1944), 81.

9. Culmination

1. Tim Hilton, *Manchester Guardian Weekly* (October 9, 1988).

10. Aftermath

1. For Homer and transparent watercolor in the Adirondacks, see Judith Walsh, "Innovation in Homer's Late Watercolors," in Nicoli Cikovsky Jr. and Franklin Kelly, *Winslow Homer, National Gallery of Art* (New Haven: Yale Univ. Press, 1996), 283–99.

Bibliography

Adamson, William. *Notices of the Services of the 27th Northumberland Light Infantry Militia*. Newcastle upon Tyne: Robert Robinson, 1877.

Athens, Elizabeth, Brandon Rudd, and Martha Tedeschi. *Coming Away: Winslow Homer in England*. New Haven: Yale Univ. Press, 2017.

Carr, Lorraine. "Cullercoats and Whitley 1895." *Ordnance Survey Map*, Sheet 889.04. Rev. ed. Leadgate Consett, Northumberland: Alan Godfrey Maps, 1919.

Citkovski, Nicolai Jr., and Franklin Kelly. *Winslow Homer*. New Haven: Yale Univ. Press, 1996.

Cross, William R. *Homer at the Beach: A Marine Painter's Journey 1869–1880*. Gloucester, MA: Cape Ann Museum, 2019.

"Coursing in America." *The Illustrated American*, April 1896, 430–31.

Downes, William Howe. *The Life and Work of Winslow Homer*. Boston: Houghton Mifflin, 1911.

Giese, Lucretia Hoover. "Winslow Homer's 'Better Painting': *Old Woman Gathering Faggots*, 1865." *Visual Resources* 27, no. 1 (2011): 63–76.

Goodrich, Lloyd, and Abigail Booth Gerdts. *Record of Works by Winslow Homer*. Vol. 4.1. New York: Homer Art Education Project, 2005–2014.

Goodrich, Lloyd. *The Graphic Art of Winslow Homer*. New York: Museum of Graphic Art, 1968.

———. *Winslow Homer*. New York: Macmillan, 1944.

Graham, Hugh. "Storm Watching." *Times of London*, Travel Section, October 26, 2010.

Harrison, Tony. *Winslow Homer in England*. Ocean Park, ME: Hornby Editions, 2004.

Hilton, Tim. "Review." *Manchester Guardian Weekly*, London, October 9, 1888.

Knipe, Tony, ed. *Winslow Homer: All the Cullercoats Pictures*. Sunderland, UK: Northern Centre for Contemporary Art, 1988.

———, ed. *Winslow Homer: All the Cullercoats Pictures*. Sunderland, UK: Northern Centre for Contemporary Art, 1988.

McCombie, Grace, ed. "Newcastle and Gateshead." In *Architectural Guides*, edited by Nicolas Pevsner. London: Penguin, 2009.

Nairn, Ian. "Superlative Newcastle-Upon-Tyne." Originally published in *The Observer*, 1960. Edited and republished with an introduction by Owen Hatherley as *Nairn's Towns*. London: Notting Hill Editions, 2013.

Newton, Laura, with Abigail Gerdts. *Cullercoats, A North East Colony of Artists Cullercoats*. Bristol: Sansom & Co., 2003.

————, eds. *Painting at the Edge: British Coastal Art Colonies 1880–1930*. Bristol: Sansom & Co., 2005.

Pevsner, Nicolas. *Northumberland*. London: Penguin, 1957.

Reed, Lloyd G. *Cullercoats Village 1292–1950*. Raleigh, NC: Lulu Editions, 2014.

Remington, Frederic. "Coursing Rabbits on the Plains." *Outlook*, May 1887, 111–21.

Tatham, David. *Winslow Homer in London*. Syracuse: Syracuse Univ. Press, 2010.

————. *Winslow Homer and the Pictorial Press*. Syracuse: Syracuse Univ. Press, 2003.

Tomlinson, William Weaver. *Historical Notes on Cullercoats, Whitley and Monkseaton, with a Descriptive Memoir of the Coast from Tynemouth to St. Mary's Island*. London: Walter Scott, Ltd., 1893.

————. *The North Eastern Railway: Its Rise and Development*. Devon: Newton Abbott, 1915.

Van Rensselaer, Marianna Griswold. "An American Artist in England." *The Century*, November 1883, 13–21.

————. "The Watercolor Exhibition, New York." *American Architect and Building News*, March 12, 1883, 138.

Walsh, Judith. "Innovation in Homer's Late Watercolors." In Nicoli Cikovsky Jr. and Franklin Kelly, *Winslow Homer, National Gallery of Art*. New Haven: Yale Univ. Press, 1996, 283–99.

————. "More Skillful, More Refined, More Delicate: England." In *Watercolors by Winslow Homer: The Color of Light*, edited by Martha Tedeschi and Kristi Dahm, with contributions by Judith Walsh and Karen Huang. Chicago: Art Institute of Chicago, 2006, 76–110.

Index

Italic page numbers denote illustrations.

Adamson, Alan, 22–23
Adamson, Bryan, 83n13
Adamson, Hannah, 22
Adamson, William, 33–34
Adamson Memorial, 83–84n13
Albert, Prince of England, 20
American exhibitions of Homer's Culler-coats work, 7
American Watercolor Society, 7
Anglo-Saxon England, 12

Beloit Daily Call, 22
Bland, Archdeacon, 12
British Museum, 12

Carrick, Jane, 22
Carrick, Thomas, 20–21
Century, The, 8
cobles, 10
cobles racing, 32
Cochrane, Sir Cecil, 12
Cross, William, 84n1
Cullercoats: Art Colony, 12, 24; Cliff House, 19; commuters, 22; fishing fleet, 18; map of, *16*; the "Sands," 10; village, *17*; Watch House, *ii*, *17*

Downes, William Howe, 3, 81n3
Durham Cathedral, 13

Elizabeth I, Queen of England, 81n4
Emmerson, Henry Hetherington, 84n4

fisherfolk: misdescribed as peasants, 4, 81n4; origins of, 18; as product of Industrial Revolution, 81n4
fishermen, painted by Homer, 26
fishing trawlers, 31
fishwives, 26, 27

Garibaldi, Giuseppe, 14; Homer's portrait of, 15
Gerdts, Abigail Booth, 32
Giese, Lucretia Hoover, 9
Goodrich, Lloyd, 2, 48

Hadrian's Wall, 12, 23
Homer, Charles Jr. (brother), 2
Homer, Winslow: as autodidact, 9; and Cullercoats fisherfolk, 1, 2; Cullercoats manner, 1; Cullercoats residences, 18–19; Cullercoats subjects, 7; death, 2, 77; in France, 2; freedom from convention, 8; as greatest painter of sea, 3; Houghton Farm paintings, 5; in London, 1–2; as "most American of American painters," 1; as National Academy of Design member, 24; as "new artist," 1, 7, 9; New York exhibitions

Homer, Winslow (*cont.*)
  of Cullercoats paintings, 2, 67; powers
    of observation, 9; Royal Academy, 63;
    "turning points," 3; unacademic and
    naive qualities, 13; work ethic, 11
Homer, Winslow (works): *Adirondack
    Guide*, 76; *An Afterglow*, *45*, 67; *Beach
    Scene, Cullercoats*, 30, *37*, 49; *The
    Breakwater, Cullercoats*, *38*, 50, 52, 71;
    Bridlington Quay, 30, *41*, 61; *Cloud
    Shadows*, 75; *The Cotton Pickers*, 63;
    Coursing the Hare, *40*, 59–61; *Dressing
    for the Carnival*, 26; *Eight Bells*, 76;
    Fisherfolk on the Beach at Cullercoats,
    37, 47; *Fisher Girl*, 76; *A Fisherman's
    Family*, 29; *Flamborough Head*, 61;
    Four Fishwives, 30, 33, *36*, 67, 69; *The
    Gale (The Coming Away of the Gale)*,
    40, 56–57, 71–75; *Hark! The Lark*,
    42, 68; *Homecoming*, 30, *36*; *Houses of
    Parliament*, 59; *The Incoming Tide*, *43*,
    67, 69; *Inside the Bar*, *44*, 67, 69–71;
    The Life Brigade, 19; *The Life Line*,
    45, 48, 64, 74–75; *The Lookout*, *38*,
    51–52; *Men Beaching a Boat*, 20, *35*;
    Mending the Nets, 29; *Mink Pond*, 76;
    An October Day, 76; *Passing a Wreck—
    Mid Ocean*, 85n3; *Perils of the Sea*,
    39, 54; *Promenade on the Beach*, 33;
    Returning Fishing Boats, *44*, 67; *Sail-
    ing Home at Sunset*, 71; *Shepherdesses
    Resting*, 29; *A Summer Night*, 76; *The
    Two Guides*, 76; *Undertow*, 76; *A Voice
    from the Cliffs*, *43*, 67–69; **Watching
    from the Cliffs**, 28–29, *35*; **Watching the
    Tempest**, *39*, 55; *Windy Day, **Culler-
    coats***, 70; *The Wreck of the **Iron Crown***,
    74–75
Humber River, 13

Jefferson, James, 62
Jefferson, Margaret (Maggie), **26–27**, 30,
    62–64, 72

Newcastle upon Tyne, 18; map **of**, *23*
Northeastern Railway, 14
Northumberland, Dukes of, 13

Pearson, John Loughborough, **13**
Percy, Algernon George, Duke **of** Nor-
    thumberland, 13
Port of Tyne, 23

Royal Academy, New York, 63
Royal Academy of Arts, London, 11
Royal National Lifeboat Institute, 18–19,
    21

"Scotch mists," 47

Tomlinson, William Weaver, 2
Turner, J. M. W., 12

Van Rensselaer, Mariana, 7–8, 12–14

David Tatham was born in Wellesley, Massachusetts, and educated at the University of Massachusetts–Amherst and Syracuse University. In 1962 he joined the faculty of Syracuse University's Department of Fine Arts (now the Department of Art and Music Histories), attaining in 2002 the rank of professor emeritus. He is the author of books, exhibition catalogues, and many scholarly articles concerning painting, sculpture, and the graphic arts in nineteenth- and twentieth-century North America. His numerous studies of the life and work of Winslow Homer include four earlier volumes published by Syracuse University Press: *Winslow Homer and the Illustrated Book* (1992), *Winslow Homer in the Adirondacks* (1996), *Winslow Homer and the Pictorial Press* (2003), and *Winslow Homer in London* (2010).

Other Studies of Winslow Homer by David Tatham
Published by Syracuse University Press

Winslow Homer and the Illustrated Book (1992)

Winslow Homer in the Adirondacks (1996)

Winslow Homer and the Pictorial Press (2003)

Winslow Homer in London: A New York Artist Abroad (2010)